SIMPLY
SCRIPTURE
for Lent and Easter

"Reading this book, I felt like Colleen Vermeulen was speaking straight from her heart to mine as she took me through the very basic, practical steps of learning to love the Bible and pray with it. This is one of the best introductions to daily Bible reading and prayer I have come across. I highly recommend it both for Bible beginners and the biblically literate who would like to learn to pray with scripture."

John Bergsma
Author of *Bible Basics for Catholics*

"An impactful, approachable, 'back to basics' guide for prayer! This guide takes the guesswork out of the question 'How do I pray this Lent?' by providing a daily framework to reflect on scripture. The focus on the Gospel of Mark is fitting, as a large portion of this gospel highlights events in the week leading up to Christ's Passion. Catholics of all stages can benefit from this invitation to walk step-by-step with Jesus and the disciples this Lent and Easter."

Kassie Manning
Cofounder of Every Sacred Sunday

"This book is the perfect guide for walking through scripture during Lent and Easter. It's both beautiful and practical—an excellent companion for any family looking to dive deeper into the Bible and grow in liturgical living!"

Jason and Rachel Bulman
National speakers and hosts of *Meet the Bulmans*

"*Simply Scripture for Lent and Easter* is not just for families. It is for anyone, beginner or Bible expert, who wants to enrich their prayer time with scripture or turn their Bible reading into prayer."

From the foreword by Sarah Christmyer
General editor of *Living the Word Catholic Women's Bible*

SIMPLY
SCRIPTURE
for Lent and Easter

A Daily Guide to Reading the Bible

Gospel of Mark and Acts of the Apostles

Colleen Reiss Vermeulen

AVE MARIA PRESS AVE Notre Dame, Indiana

Contents

Foreword

When I was growing up, reading scripture was as important to our family as going to church, and maybe more so. Of course, we were Protestants, and as such, the Bible was where we went to be with Jesus. We went there for guidance, for strength, for encouragement, and for the words to help us pray. It was the starting place for our personal devotions, the focus of mealtime prayers, the subject of personal study, and the focal point of lots of family conversations. And when I floundered as a teenager, it was the Bible and prayer that pulled me through.

Becoming Catholic, which I did early in my marriage, gave me serious culture shock. I loved the way scripture permeated the Mass and the prayers and the theology. But Catholic devotions were a mystery to me. I did not know how to practice my faith without putting the Bible front and center—and it seemed to me that Catholics kept the Bible in the background, if not in the closet. How could I replace weekly Bible study with a weekly Rosary group? How could I hang on to what was precious to me, maintaining my daily time in the Bible, and at the same time adopt things like daily Mass or praying the Divine Office? How would I find time, and how would they all fit together? And what habits should I teach our children?

Today, as my children raise little ones of their own, I am grateful for the resources now available—including the book you are holding in your hands. Many wonderful Bibles and Bible studies encourage reading and praying with scripture in light of Catholic teaching; others show you how to get more out of the readings at Mass. Colleen Vermeulen's *Simply Scripture* merges both traditions in a way that is solidly Catholic. Starting within the familiar context of the Divine Office, it uses that easy rhythm of daily prayer to frame a consecutive read-through of a whole book of the Bible. The psalms and Collect prayer facilitate prayerful listening; simple questions foster conversation with the Lord; and the continuous reading through of a book helps you take in pieces of scripture within the context of the whole, improving understanding.

In the process, daily prayer becomes a meeting place for ongoing conversation: a way to know and talk with God by listening to his Word.

Simply Scripture is so simple that the whole family can do it together. Children can get to know the real Bible—not just a Bible story book—hear God speak to them, and learn to engage with what they hear. There is just enough commentary to provide a basic understanding, and the reflection and discussion prompts can be answered simply or in depth. But *Simply Scripture* is not just for families. It is for anyone, beginner or Bible expert, who wants to enrich their prayer time with scripture or turn their Bible reading into prayer. It is an invitation to a deeper knowledge of the Father, who in the Bible "meets His children with great love and speaks with them" (*Dei Verbum*, 21).

As you read and pray with *Simply Scripture*, listen to God's heart as you open your heart to him.

Sarah Christmyer
General Editor, *Living the Word Catholic Women's Bible*

Acknowledgments

My deepest thanks goes first and foremost to Luke, my husband. Without his deep friendship, partnership, and giving of time and energy to our household, I would have never had the opportunity to say yes to an invitation to write a book. Secondly, I am grateful for the presence of our oldest two sons, Peter and Cyril, who were the catalysts for a prayer time that was of and for our entire family.

At the start of Advent in 2020, we decided to substitute a continuous reading through the Gospel of Mark for the more seasonal, daily scripture passage in a Liturgy of the Hours-style family prayer book we had been using for a few years. Two of our local dioceses, the Diocese of Lansing and Archdiocese of Detroit, were promoting daily Bible reading plans—so we took that up in spirit but knew we needed to slow it down and simplify it if it was going to be something our five- and seven-year-olds could genuinely participate in.

We began reading the Gospel of Mark, straight through, and Peter and Cyril eagerly latched onto the concrete sense of accomplishment and the drama of a continuous narrative. Years prior, *really* reading the Bible and getting to know books in full had been a fruitful step in my own relationship with God, so I was not surprised by the positive impact on our kids' engagement in prayer.

As we finished the Gospel of Mark, Peter declared, "And now it's my turn to pick a book, right? I'm picking Luke's Gospel because it has Christmas in it." A habit was born. Many months later, Cyril got his chance to select the next book (he chose the Gospel of John). Then came my husband's turn to pick (Letter to the Hebrews), and then "we" made a group choice to do Acts of the Apostles next, in honor of our third son, toddler Paul. Our youngest son, baby Francis, got his first pick (Habbakuk) by virtue of a random drawing.

Throughout the past almost four years of this family habit, Peter and Cyril's practice of prayer and discussion was the starting point for what became this book. And, Luke reminded me, when it came time to write these acknowledgements, "Thank Peter and Cyril for not closing windows on the computer before you hit save."

Beyond my family, my gratitude extends in a special way to:

Fred Morath and Cathryn Torgerson-Wade, who welcomed me into the Catholic Biblical School's ministry of adult faith formation, which provides a powerful example of the fruit that comes when we sincerely seek God in his Word. This book provides a taste of the Catholic Biblical School (catholicbiblicalschool.org) at home for daily prayer. Thanks also to Katrina Iamarino, Susan Schudt, and Beth Spizarny, who each provided a providential sign or confirming word as this book developed.

Sarah Christmyer and Heidi Hess Saxton, who first took interest in how we were making the Bible part of family prayer time, and who saw the need for all Catholics to have an accessible way to not just read, but truly *pray* the Bible.

Barbara Morgan (1938–2019), whom I served as an assistant to for two years. Although my job description in working for her was focused on children's catechesis, when opportunities to teach God's Word to adults arose, she assuredly said that I "must" teach the scriptures because it feeds one's soul. She was, of course, correct. Thanks also to the many Catechesis of the Good Shepherd catechists whom I've observed and assisted. You model loving trust that direct contact with the inspired Word of God bears fruit when we guide and get out of the way!

Jennifer Guarneri Beil, who first moved me to curiosity about things eternal and actively brought me along in proclaiming the Gospel to others; Pastors Bryan Miller and David Page, who when I asked them about difficult to interpret Bible passages as an emerging adult, resisted giving simplistic answers and instead encouraged me to ask God what it means; and Kenneth and Barbara Eldridge, who acted as "Barnabas" in my life (Acts 11:25–26) calling me into disciple-making ministry.

The notes that became this book were written in the midst of daily life, visiting extended family (thank you for engaging our children!), waiting on the side of Catechesis of Good Shepherd atriums, at parks and museums, and in our kitchen. Gratitude beyond words to our God, who provides, sustains, and illumines, so that we can be his witnesses, wherever we find ourselves.

Colleen Reiss Vermeulen
May 12, 2024
Solemnity of the Ascension

Introduction

If you're reading this book, at *some* point in your life you may have had that surprising, sometimes exciting, sometimes joyful, and sometimes scary experience of saying to Jesus, "Yes, Lord. I have come to believe that *you* are the Messiah, the Son of God, the one who is coming into the world" (Jn 11:27, NABRE; emphasis mine). If not, I hope that by the time you finish reading it, you will!

Of course, it's one thing to know that Jesus is Lord in your mind and heart, but *what comes next?* How does that relationship with him begin to grow?

I'm so glad you asked. Let me tell you how it happened for me.

I grew up in a practicing, Catholic family, but it was not until my late teens that I came to believe that Jesus really was *the* Lord, and that he was the Messiah, the one specially anointed and chosen by God to *save*, and to save *even me* (a respectable, well-behaved, get-good-grades-and-volunteer-in-community kind of young woman whom most of society wouldn't view as in need of "saving"). Pope Benedict XVI called this kind of encounter with Jesus, and acknowledgment of who Jesus truly is, "the fundamental decision" of one's life, something that "gives life a new horizon and a decisive direction" (*Deus Caritas Est*, 1). But what comes next?

I might start to call myself a disciple (follower) of Jesus, but how do I actually get to know this person whom I have decided to follow? How do I come to see those new horizons and new directions? How do I come to know more of who God is and understand his plans? How do I even get through my daily troubles and challenges?

The answer is, most simply, prayer. Prayer is where my desire to personally know God (and his plans, directions, guidance, etc.) and God's desire to intimately know me overlap. Prayer is that meeting place; prayer *is* our relationship with God (see *CCC*, 2560, 2558). How does one begin to pray—and to really mean it?

One of the best ways to come to understand the mind and heart of God is through scripture (as the title of this book, *Simply Scripture*, suggests)—through the careful, prayerful reading of the Word of God. The gospels are a particularly good place to start this journey, for they offer the life story of Jesus, God's perfect revelation of himself to us. And so in this book we will explore the Gospel of Mark as well as the story of the first Christians, told in Acts of the Apostles.

In Luke's gospel, we find that Jesus's first disciples (who were familiar with the memorized prayers of their Jewish faith and scriptures) saw the way Jesus prayed to God, the true relationship between the Son and Father, and responded with expectation, "Lord, teach *us* to pray" (Lk 11:1; emphasis mine). Prayer is simple, but it isn't easy. It's not just you and me who struggle with it!

Immediately after introducing the "life of prayer" in the *Catechism of the Catholic Church*, the Church proceeds to reflect on this "battle of prayer," observing that throughout the ages God's children have always experienced challenges like reducing prayer to ritual and rote memorization, being stressed about not finding the time to pray, finding prayer irrelevant to our daily lives, and just feeling flat-out discouraged as a *failure* for experiencing dryness or distraction in prayer (see *CCC*, 2725–2733). For me, the greatest struggle over my past two decades of prayer has been the listening part: knowing that God is speaking to me enough that I *want* to pray each day, rather than praying out of duty because I know I should.

From Distraction to Simplicity

There are many ways to pray, and since prayer is relationship with God, the nuances of each individual's prayer life will be unique. There are *so many* ways to pray that are part of Catholic spirituality; in our modern era of books and digital resources, we can have access to nearly anything we want. Even so, we often get stuck when trying to "improve" our prayer lives. Friends (both on social media and in person) offer us a myriad of suggestions for how to pray. The sheer number of choices can seem flat-out overwhelming, or as though we're not "good" Catholics if we're not praying a certain devotional from the Church's treasury of practices.

The truth is, there is no single prayer that is guaranteed to usher us into a genuine, authentic relationship with God. Indeed, the sheer number of choices on offer can actually make it harder for a person to feel confident and content in his or her own prayer life. Too much "stuff" can get in the way of our ultimate goal: a two-way conversation between God and me, alternately speaking and listening.

So what's the best way to get back to basics? The Church teaches that the Holy Spirit guides us, as God's beloved children, to two specific, concrete "wellsprings" of prayers: the Word of God and the liturgy, "where Christ awaits us to enable us to drink of the Holy Spirit" (*CCC*, 2652; see also 2653–2655). So if I'm struggling to find motivation, meaning, and time to pray, I ought to go to the sources the Church recommends to find my life-giving foundation for prayer. Before I overcomplicate my prayer life and get discouraged, stressed, or burdened by comparing myself to others, I should seek refuge and freedom by simply embracing the nourishing foundation the Church points me to—the *wellsprings* of scripture and liturgy.

The Wellspring of Scripture: Listening by Reading

Sometimes we overlook the sacred scriptures as an essential part of prayer. I can glance at the sheer size of a Bible on my shelf and think, "Meh, most of that is probably boring and hard to read." Or I might say, "I get enough of the Bible at Mass" or "I'm not an intellectual, the scriptures are head knowledge, and I just want to connect my heart to God."

But here's the wonderful, amazing reality: just as God gives his very self to us through the food of the Eucharist—a human way of nourishing us—God also gives his very self to us in the words of scripture. God knows our human nature (and even experiences being fully human, having becoming flesh himself) and understands that words are part of our nature. We understand words with precision and depth in a way no other created species in the known universe does! Our delight in being known and knowing others through language is part of being human.

God does not want to be a remote, abstract Creator who hides himself from us. On the contrary, God gives himself to us in the scriptures so that we can hear him, discover his plans for us, and have a real relationship with him through the Bible. While some people experience locutions (meaning hearing an audible voice of God) or dazzling, symbolic visions in prayer, these extraordinary events are not the only way God communicates with us. A simple, accessible *wellspring* for hearing God speak to us is praying with the Bible. As a wellspring, the scriptures are the *primary* (from which all others flow!) and *abounding* source. God's power to speak through them will never run out—we're never going to become so mature as disciples of Jesus Christ that we've moved "beyond" the Bible.

The Wellspring of Liturgy: Flowing from Mass to the World

The Liturgy of the Hours is the name for the "public prayer of the Church," the liturgy that is intended for you and me in the midst of our ordinary lives (see *CCC*, 1174–1175). The Liturgy of the Hours draws its form and substance from the earliest days of the Church and offers a way to not just read the scriptures but *read them as prayer*, allowing each of us to do as the Church encourages, to "seek in reading and . . . find in meditating" (*CCC*, 2654) on the Word of God—the Bible.

The wisdom of the Church reveals that, at its core, our prayer life doesn't need to be fancy or innovative. It can be *simply scripture*, prayed as the Church guides us in her liturgy, as a dialogue between God and us. That dialogue is intended for each of us—not just "super holy people" like the great theologians and saints. As St. Ambrose wrote, "We speak to him when we pray; we listen to him when we read the divine oracles [scriptures]" (quoted in *CCC*, 2653).

Growing from a Wellspring

You're invited to step into a journey, across the Lent and Easter seasons, to pray the scriptures simply. During Jesus's time of mission preparation in the desert (the origin of our season of Lent), he was filled with the Holy Spirit (see Lk 4:1, 14).* When Jesus's earliest followers received the Holy Spirit fifty days after Easter, they too set out on mission accompanied by *simply scripture*, as

---

Note: * Lent originated as a season of preparation for baptism, a sacrament that unites us to Jesus Christ in a way that we share in his ministry (see CCC, 897).

catechisms and modern devotionals did not yet exist.* Grounding your own prayer life, even if just for the seasons of Lent and Easter, in simplicity creates a space for the Holy Spirit's wellspring to refresh and nourish your soul.

I came to realize the power of these wellsprings myself *not* because I have a "great" prayer life (whatever that looks like!) but because I've struggled with the question of how to pray. As a teenager, I started out with prayer by asking God in my own words for things I needed or wanted, or praying for other people or specific intentions. A few years later, at a time in my life when I wasn't sure if I truly believed what the Church taught, I was browsing around the Christianity section of a Barnes & Noble bookstore and spotted the Anglican *Book of Common Prayer, 1559*. I was intrigued!

Instead of giving me essays on the spiritual life from canonized saints or devotional reflections written by someone else—in both cases, content that seemed *so* much more holy, devout, and filled with "religious" language than my own thoughts—this prayer book guided me to simply scripture, surrounded and embedded in the Christian liturgical traditions. I had to read more of the Bible and have a conversation with God *myself* rather than reading words that were the fruit of *other* people's prayer lives.

A few years later, when pondering what compact books to bring with me for an army deployment to Iraq (because I didn't have a lot of packing space), I chose a Bible and a copy of *Christian Prayer*, the Catholic, one-volume version of the Liturgy of the Hours. I was coming to realize that no amount of (even prayerful) reading of the spiritual reflections of others was a substitute for simply placing myself before God, directly in these wellsprings of prayer. Filling my mind with the prayerful reflections of someone else could become a feel-good substitute for that vulnerability and humility of putting my own heart and mind before God. Rather than read about God and about prayer without actually praying myself, I challenged myself to put more of my true self into prayer.

But here's the catch: even trying to use the Liturgy of the Hours just once a day was quite a *gush* from the wellsprings of scripture and liturgy—so much of an overflowing gush that the temptation to "just do it; just say the words"

Note: * See Acts 4:24–31 for one of the earliest examples of Jesus's followers praying. Notice that they incorporate scripture and their own words of response.

crept in. What was more important? A sense of "finishing," that I had accomplished prayer for the day? Or that I was actually conversing with God? The Church in her collective wisdom knows this temptation throughout the ages well, explaining, "Through his Word, God speaks to man. By words, mental or vocal, our prayer takes flesh. Yet it is most important that the heart should be present to him to whom we are speaking in prayer: 'Whether or not our prayer is heard depends not on the number of words, but on the fervor of our souls'" (St. John Chrysostom, quoted in *CCC*, 2700).

This temptation to "just get through" too many words amplified itself as I became a mother and practical opportunities for quiet time in my life naturally decreased. If I wasn't going to be able to "fix" my prayer life by returning to the days of having lots of quiet time as a single young adult, it would need to be of a higher quality. I needed to simply pray, to balance out the words of scripture with the true presence of my heart, what the Church calls contemplation ("a gaze of faith fixed on Jesus, an attentiveness to the Word of God, a silent love") and meditation (a "quest engaging thought, imagination, [and] emotion"; *CCC*, 2723–2724). So I followed the advice of my former pastor, Fr. Michael Heintz, who said, "I tell people that the way to start praying *with* the Church in the Liturgy of the Hours is to take a tiny portion, even as small as just the Our Father, and, only when that is a habit, expand."

During those same years I began serving as an in-person teacher with the Catholic Biblical School of Michigan's adult faith formation ministry (for more information on this ministry, see page 161). Instead of holding Bible studies with excerpts on a theme or single-book studies, this ministry was *simply scripture*. The ministry invited adults to a realistically paced journey through every book of the Bible in full, with personal talks from a real teacher—an instructor with the heart of a catechist—bringing the scriptures to life, showing their organic unity, and revealing Catholic teaching and liturgy as flowing from the Word of God. The unity of the scriptures as a whole and the *unity of each book* of the Bible, each carefully crafted by an inspired human author responding to the Holy Spirit, powerfully impacted my prayers and the prayers of the hundreds of adults I met.

I realized that when we limit ourselves to short excerpts or jump around too much in the Bible, it actually becomes harder to prayerfully read and understand. As Dr. Peter S. Williamson, coeditor of the Catholic Commentary on Sacred Scripture series, attests, "In the long run, it is most fruitful to work one's way through whole books of the Bible, rather than just selections."[1]

But was reading entire books of the Bible in a prayerful way good just for adult Catholics doing faith formation on the Bible? Or was it something for *everyone*? My husband and I, with our three children aged seven, five, and one, took the plunge in December 2020. For my husband and me, the decision came from a place of frustration with our family prayer life. We had felt our sense of unease with family prayer increasing as our toddlers grew into school-aged children. We found ourselves avoiding prayer more often. We flat out didn't like praying with our kids most of the time, as we thought they were "distracting" and "wasting" the time we set aside for prayer. This fueled our own sense of parental guilt at not being able to pray "well" as a family.

So we simplified and started reading the Gospel of Mark, surrounded by a little bit of the Liturgy of the Hours. By going to the *wellsprings* of scripture and liturgy, we could push away the FOMO (fear of missing out) and unrelenting pressures that told us "You're not good enough" as parents. Years later, we've grown as a family and grown in our individual relationships with God through prayer. But the foundation of *simply scripture* is always there. I know that whatever new idea I get to enrich my prayer life, I should not let it displace the foundational *wellsprings*, the living water through which the Holy Spirit quenches our thirst and refreshes us.

This book is designed as a *prompt* to prime the pump of your heart and mind so that the divine wellsprings can flow into your life during Lent and Easter and well beyond. I offer it in a spirit of humility. The most important words in this book are not from me: the truly important words are those of scripture and liturgy. My goal in writing is to offer just enough to encourage your prayers so that my prompts fade into the background as the real substance grows in the communication between you and God. When we realize that "we do not know how to pray as we ought" (Rom 8:26), we are "ready to receive freely the gift of prayer" (*CCC*, 2559). As you begin, trust that God, "who began a good work in you will bring it to completion at the day of Jesus Christ" (Phil 1:7) as we pray together, *"Come, Holy Spirit! Shape my life by the reading of God's Word!"*[2]

How to Use This Book

By a living transmission—Tradition—the Holy Spirit
in the Church teaches the children of God to pray.
—*Catechism of the Catholic Church*, 2661

It's a Day-by-Day Guide

This book is a guided, prayerful tour through the Gospel of Mark and Acts of the Apostles. Without skipping a single word of the biblical text (and even reading some words twice!), we go on a Lenten journey to the Cross of Calvary through the eyes of Mark the evangelist, who highlights the importance of making a decision of faith. He also reveals the true identity of Jesus as a Messiah who *saves* those who believe through his own act of suffering and sacrifice. Then, in the season of Easter, we continue the story of Jesus's followers, moving outward from the Cross of Jerusalem and into the wider world as God's plan of salvation and renewal begins to spread!

Each day is titled according to the liturgical calendar (e.g., Thursday after Ash Wednesday or Second Tuesday of Easter) so that you can use it from year to year. Each day follows a pattern, inspired by the Liturgy of the Hours, that keeps us from experiencing Bible reading as a burdensome penance or a pointlessly confusing endeavor. Instead, we are invited to read the Bible from the heart, to read the Bible as *prayer*, surrounded by heartfelt connections to God found in the psalms and the Church's encouragement to truly meditate on the Bible.

The daily pattern will quickly become familiar:

- *A Liturgy of the Hours psalm verse for contemplation,* which means gazing on the Lord and simply being focused and mentally present to him.

- *A citation for a passage from Mark's gospel (Lent) or Acts of the Apostles (Easter)* with a short introduction to bring you into the vivid world of first-century believers as you read directly from your favorite Catholic Bible.
- *A weekly verse to remember, inspired by the Liturgy of the Hours,* which provides an effortless way to memorize scriptures that draw us into the liturgical season.
- *A set of prompts* to engage your mind and heart in meditating on the day's Bible passage. The first prompt draws out the literal sense; the second, the spiritual sense ("God's plan"); and the third, a point of meditation ("Make it your own").
- *A concluding prayer* adapted from a Collect prayer heard at Sunday Mass during that liturgical season and traditionally used in the Liturgy of the Hours.

Praying the Bible as an Individual or with a Group

This book is designed for use in a wide variety of configurations: individuals, couples, small groups, families with children, and faith formation groups or classes of any age or level. For using this book with children, I recommend adapting the prayer prompts and questions to a more open-ended style and have included suggestions for movement, silence, music, and more that I've used with my family as our children have grown through different developmental stages in the "Next Steps" section.*

For those praying with a partner or group, certain parts will be marked in bold to distinguish a prayer leader from the other(s). For the prayer prompts, you could choose to discuss all three openly with one another or keep the final meditation prompt between yourself and God. It's also okay to mix and match

---

Note: * Our older elementary-age children embraced the idea of the pre-printed, specific questions in the book (rather than our family's habit of spontaneous, open-ended questions) because they could read them aloud themselves. They especially liked the first question, which encouraged them to go back to the Bible and find the verse that helps us see a literal sense that is key to the passage. Lesson? Know your family or classroom and do what fits best for your setting!

and use this book sometimes for prayer with another person, and sometimes as an individual.

When and Where to Pray

This guide for praying with the Bible can be used one, two, or three times a day. The two suggested prayer sections for each day are called "morning" and "evening" (creative, right?), yet could be prayed at *any* time of the day—separately or together. For some, praying first thing in the morning is a way to focus before a busy day. For others, it may work better to combine both parts ("morning" and "evening") into one sitting when you're not feeling rushed. For some, it may feel more natural to split each day's prayer into three shorter moments of pause to connect with God.

Experiment and find what times and combinations work best. It's also okay to pray one part as an individual (e.g., "morning") and one part (e.g., "evening") with someone else or in a group (such as a couple or a family). It's more important to find *some* time to pray because there's never a *perfect* time—and for most of us, never enough time, so it seems! The same principle applies to location; you may have access to a peaceful, quiet place, or you may find that the best place to pray is at a messy kitchen table with you and members of your household munching on a bedtime snack while listening to and discussing the Bible.

Prayer *is* relationship with God. Rest assured that God *wants* this time with you. Find *any* time and *any* place, and allow God to take up your offering of prayer (however imperfect or awkward it feels to you). By putting your mind and heart into the inspired Word of God through the time-tested practices of the Church's pattern of prayer (a pattern that Jesus and Jews before him used!), you are making yourself available to God, and the Holy Spirit will do the rest!

When You Miss a Day

Here are two recommendations for when you miss a day or two. I use option 1 when I'm praying through a book of the Bible by myself and option 2 when we're using this book as a family. Both work!

1. Continue with the actual liturgical day (e.g., Fourth Thursday of Easter) and read extra from Mark or Acts to fill in the verses you missed. Because you'll be understanding more of the Bible through this daily guided reading, those catch-up days may become easier than you think!

2. Continue to follow the day-by-day reading of Mark or Acts, ignoring each day's liturgical title. There's no harm in contemplating God through a psalm the Church customarily prays on a Tuesday in the Liturgy of the Hours on a Thursday instead. Any prayer, especially through the Word of God, deepens our relationship with the Lord.

Praying the Bible:
Our Daily Pattern Goes *Way, Way* Back

The elements of daily prayer and reading the Bible continuously (without skipping around) found in this book flow from the Liturgy of the Hours (also known as the Divine Office), which is the "public prayer of the Church" intended for *everyone* (*CCC*, 1174). Since the earliest Christian times, the Liturgy of the Hours has followed two Jewish customs that Jesus practiced during his earthly ministry: praying throughout the day and praying the psalms (see *Sacrosanctum Concilium*, 84).*

These ancient rhythms and styles of daily prayer are still used around the world today. Pope Paul VI wrote that the Liturgy of the Hours is the "prayer of the whole people of God" (*Laudis Canticum*) and recommended it for all, even families (*Marialis Cultus* [*Devotion to Mary*], 53).

This daily devotional offers small portions of the Liturgy of the Hours—a single daily psalm verse, a scripture passage, a responsorial verse, meditation prompts, and a closing Collect prayer—through which all who pray them are connected in a tangible way to those in Christ's Body who pray the entire Liturgy of the Hours as part of their "work" of faith. By pausing each day to engage in the Church's three forms of prayer—vocal, meditative, and contemplative—we can experience prayer as the Church describes it: a "personal relationship with the living and true God" (*CCC*, 2721, 2558).

Note: * See Mt 27:46 and Lk 23:46 for examples of Jesus praying part of a psalm from memory, and Mt 26:30 for the communal singing of a psalm.

Psalm Verse

We begin with a verse of scripture from the Book of Psalms, which was the prayer book of first-century Jews like Jesus.* Written by various human authors under the inspiration of the Holy Spirit, the psalms have been an important part of the Church's public, communal prayer since her earliest days.

I invite you to use the psalm verse to contemplate and simply be with God, our loving Creator whom we can never capture, contain, or fully describe using human words (see *CCC*, 42). Each verse, drawn from the Liturgy of the Hours, will help you to simply *be still* and connect with God on a divine, spiritual, *supernatural* level. The Church teaches that the psalms were "prayed by Christ and fulfilled in him," and when we pray them today, Christ unites God's saving work and our personal response, teaching us how to pray (see *CCC*, 2586–2587).

Contemplate

The psalm verse of the day is immediately followed by a prompt to help you enter into a brief time of contemplative prayer. Contemplative prayer is a profoundly simple expression of prayer, just *being* with God: "It is a gaze of faith fixed on Jesus, an attentiveness to the Word of God, a silent love" (*CCC*, 2724).

Starting off your day or time of prayer with a moment of stillness can be a way to reset amid your busyness, an experience of relief or calmness, and at the same time a heartfelt challenge to "let go" and let God *see* you without any barriers or masks.

Cultivating the patience of my own heart and settling my own mind to simply *be* with God has always been a challenge for me! I encourage you to start small—make it an authentic moment of stillness and silence (no matter how long or short a "moment" is for you) and then gradually expand the number of minutes you spend *gazing* upon the Lord.

If you find yourself continuously distracted, consider setting aside a notebook or journal, and write down any thoughts or concerns you want God to know about. It's time well spent in building your relationship with God and can set your heart and mind free to simply be present with the Lord.

Note: * Jesus prayed the psalms as part of his daily prayers, even quoting two from the Cross (Psalms 22 and 31).

Psalm-Prayer

In the Liturgy of the Hours, psalm-prayers are given to help understand the psalms, written about a thousand years before the birth of Jesus, through the new eternal reality of Jesus the Messiah (see *General Instruction of the Liturgy of the Hours*, 112). This prayer (prayed aloud in a group or silently as an individual) is designed to "gather up and round off the thoughts and aspirations" of those praying (see *General Instruction of the Liturgy of the Hours*, 112). The psalm-prayers offered in this book offer a closure to the psalm verse and an introduction to prepare your heart for reading the day's scripture passage.

Here are a few practical tips to help you get started:

- *If you're praying as an individual,* you could say this short prayer aloud or silently.
- *If you're praying with one or more other people,* have one person say aloud the initial part of the verse written in plain text (e.g., for Ash Wednesday, "Happy is he whose help is in the God of Jacob") and then all others reply with the **bolded** text ("**whose hope is in the Lord his God**"). The opening psalm verses serve to invite the Holy Spirit into prayer time; through the responsive style of reading in a pair or group, you invite one another to come join in this special time.
- *If you're dividing the day's prayer into multiple sessions,* the psalm-prayer itself *or* the psalm-prayer followed by the daily Bible passage are both good ways to "end" the morning (or first) time of prayer. By giving the passage a first read, you may find that the Holy Spirit speaks to you throughout the day, bringing questions and connections to your life to mind.

Enter the Word of God

Reading books of the Bible in full, continuously (without skipping around), might seem unusual or even a little intimidating! However, the truth is that God chose real humans to be the authors of the various books of the Bible. God didn't choose these people by accident, so Catholics believe that the sacred scriptures have both divine *and* human authors.

Through the inspiration of the Holy Spirit, real human authors who lived in specific times and places wrote complete books—not just excerpts or summary stories. Reading a book in full actually makes the Bible *more* understandable. Think of your favorite fiction or nonfiction books—how difficult might they be to understand if you only read excerpts or skipped around without following the author's order and design? When we humans write, we each do it with our own style. By reading a book in full, you're acquainting yourself with that human author's style—his way of making introductions, his method of transitioning between different settings or ideas, and his internal, logical flow of drama or tensions within the book.

To set the stage for each day's reading, I offer some brief comments on the historical setting, culture of the time, and teachings of the Church that have helped me truly enter into the world of the first century and start to really *understand* what the Bible is saying (instead of just trying to "get through it" or read it for the sake of reading and check a box). My aim is to serve *your* listening to God's Word, rather than give you my opinions, applications, or personal reflections. Reading the Bible continuously, as part of the Liturgy of the Hours, comes from the traditional practice of monastic or contemplative religious communities.[1] When you read the Bible continuously, you never have to worry about taking it out of context! Whether you read the daily passage from Mark or Acts in the morning, during the day (lunch break), or in the evening, the goal is to enter into the Bible with your heart wide open.

The sacred scriptures are an incredible gift of God's desire to meet us and have a relationship with us as human beings. Just as God sent his Son, Jesus, to experience all of the ups and downs and *reality* of human existence with us, the scriptures are God choosing to communicate with us in a way we as human beings seem designed to relate to—through words and real-life events!

My short introduction to each day's reading is followed by the chapters and verses for the day, from the Gospel of Mark (Lent) and Acts of the Apostles (Easter). The full text of the passage is *not* printed in this book so that you can choose the edition, translation, and format of the Bible that works best for you (more on this in "Practical Tips for Reading Scripture"). The daily passage is designed to be short enough that you can remember most of what you've read as you ponder the questions and prayer prompts that follow. Sometimes, I will repeat some verses across multiple days so that you don't forget the setting of and lead-in to an event. When you miss a day, it's okay to combine readings from previous days.

During the season of Lent, our readings from Mark's gospel are wholly different from the lectionary readings for Sunday and weekday Masses (even in Year B of the lectionary cycle, when Mark's gospel is used during Ordinary Time, there are just a handful of selections from his gospel during Lent).

During the season of Easter, the Church reads a significant portion of Acts of the Apostles within Sunday and weekday Masses. The daily guided readings in this book are similar to the lectionary, with adjustments to allow for the full reading of Acts of the Apostles.

Practical Tips for Reading Scripture

Picking a Bible (or Bibles!)

We are blessed to live in an age where we can find excerpts of the Bible everywhere, from mini-magazines to smartphone apps. But having and using a full-sized Bible (or at a minimum, a New Testament) whenever possible brings us into concrete contact with the physicality of the Word of God.

The Bible itself is even a *sacramental*, the Church's term for sacred signs that bear resemblance to the sacraments and signify positive spiritual effects (see *CCC*, 1667). Using a Bible, rather than a book containing excerpts, allows your eyes to drift naturally to what comes before and after a particular day's passage, so you won't miss the important context clues like timing and places. It also makes it possible to notice cross-references to other Bible passages and helpful background content your Bible's editor may have included.

If you don't already have a Catholic Bible you enjoy reading, explore the many options available! For example, you might seek out an adult-level Catholic study Bible because the supplemental notes will be more extensive and help you gain background understanding on the text or even answer questions others might ask. If reading with a family, you might seek out an edition of the Bible designed for children or youth so that the supplemental content is targeted toward the age levels of your family. You might seek out an edition that has extra space for notetaking so that you can record the insights you have during prayer; for example, *The Ave Catholic Notetaking Bible* and the *Living the Word Catholic Women's Bible*, available through Ave Maria Press, both have wide margins and are cross-referenced to the *Catechism*, which can be helpful if you desire to expand your reflection on the spiritual senses of scripture.

Find the Bible that works for you. (And remember, it's okay to experiment and use more than one Bible!) Whatever Bible you choose, be ready to write, since even without a notetaking Bible, underlining and highlighting is an excellent way to take in key details and remember the words and phrases the Holy Spirit is drawing your heart and mind to.

How Many Times to Read the Daily Bible Passage?

This is up to you. If you're praying in one session per day, then reading the passage once will enable you to respond immediately in prayer—and if in a group, in discussion. If you're praying in two sessions per day, you might find it useful to end your first session (for many of us, our "morning" prayer) with a *first* reading of the passage so that the Holy Spirit can bring connections or phrases to your mind throughout the day, and then reread the passage to begin your second ("evening") prayer time. Or, if you're praying in two sessions but are short on time in the morning (our mornings as a family are *rushed*, for sure—we do not attempt any sort of longer, focused prayer!), I'd recommend saving your reading of the passage until that "evening" or second prayer time of the day.

Praying with Others

If you're praying with others, I recommend having someone with a good read-ing voice read the commentary and then the Bible passage aloud. If there are too many people to share a single Bible, do have enough Bibles so that everyone has access to a Bible for reviewing the passage during discussion.

Verse to Remember

In the Liturgy of the Hours, the Bible passage is followed by a responsorial verse (also called a responsory), meaning a short phrase of scripture that is intended to "enable God's word to sink deeper into mind and heart" (*General Instruction of the Liturgy of the Hours*, 172). In this book, immediately following the day's Bible passage, I offer a weekly verse to remember that draws us toward the major themes of the daily readings and the liturgical season. Because it is weekly, you and those you pray with will (painlessly!) begin to memorize it, and so by the end of a liturgical season you may have gained a handful of new "memory" verses of the Bible written on your heart and mind. If memorizing does not come easily to you, do not worry. The point is not to memorize; the point is to pray—to listen to God and speak to him from your heart.

Practical Tips

If you're praying with more than one person, have one person say aloud the initial part of the verse written in plain text (e.g., for Ash Wednesday, "Repent and believe in the Good News") and then all others reply with the **bolded** text

("**The kingdom of God is at hand**"). If you're praying as an individual, you could say this short prayer aloud or silently.

Respond to God's Word

In the Liturgy of the Hours, the time following the scripture reading is called "Respond to God's Word" and includes silence and/or a short homily. Most of us think of the word *homily* as something that happens at Mass—something a priest or deacon says to us—but in the original Greek, where the word *homily* comes from, *homilía* often referred to an explanation, discussion, or conversation about scripture.

When you discuss, with others or with God in prayer, what you just heard during the reading—what the words or events might mean, what intrigues you about the passage, and how the Holy Spirit is speaking in your mind or heart—that is in a sense a homily. Opening our hearts and minds to hear God's voice speaking to us in our ordinary lives is our *response* to God's invitation to friendship and conversation.

As St. Gregory the Great wrote, "Scripture is like a river . . . broad and deep, shallow enough here for the lamb to go wading, but deep enough there for the elephant to swim."[2] Whether you find yourself individually engaging in mental prayer to search the scriptures or discussing with a partner or group, the unifying and most important thing is to allow the Holy Spirit to speak to *you*. Reading and praying with the Bible can be intimidating if we think we need to "know" everything about the Bible. Not only is this impossible (since the sacred scriptures are *infinite* in their depth and profundity!), but also it's actually unhelpful.

Our humility and openness to hearing and seeing what God wants to show us are what make us "good" pray-ers and readers of the scriptures. Some days, you might choose to stick to the three prompts I have provided. Other days, the Holy Spirit might provide you with a personal prompt, specific to an event in your life or an emotion you're experiencing. Listen to those movements of the Holy Spirit and follow them. The Holy Spirit is the Lord of *life*, who knows how to speak to each of us in a way that uniquely fits our personality and season of life. For some of us, it's through our emotions and an "obvious" spiritual connection. For others, it's through a curiosity about the mention of a random fact that draws us into the scriptures where the Lord desires to speak to us.

God's "voice" doesn't always sound like a loudspeaker in one's ear. I like the acronym FRUIT for considering how God might be speaking: how I **F**eel, **R**espond/Reply, **U**nderstand, **I**magine, and **T**hink are all ways of "hearing" God in the Bible. If you are **F**eeling, **R**esponding/Replying, **U**nderstanding (or spinning your wheels trying to understand!), **I**magining, or **T**hinking through the sacred scriptures, then you're making yourself available to the Lord. You are responding to God's Word, meditating on it, and seeking a deeper relationship with him in a meaningful way!

Practical Tips

Each day's prayer offers three questions to invite you deeper into God's Word.

- The first prompt (identified/symbolized by ﹨) draws you into the real-world, first-century setting of the scriptures. Looking carefully at the words and details helps your imagination take flight as you strive to understand how early followers of Jesus might have heard these words. This is a perfect time to use a pen, pencil, or highlighter to mark key details in your Bible.*

  When you put yourself into a first-century mindset and imagine you are present in a scene, you are coming to know what the Church calls the "literal sense" of scripture (*CCC*, 116). Don't worry about figuring out the "right" or "correct" answer. Your goal can be as simple as underlining or highlighting a detail (or many details) in your Bible that helps you understand what's going on in the scene.

- The second prompt (identified/symbolized by †) invites you to ponder what the Church calls the "spiritual senses" of scripture. To do so you build upon your understanding of the words to see God's plan of salvation through Jesus Christ and his Body, the Church, and the implications for the everlasting life God offers you as a gift, available to you right now and eternally. The Church encourages you to draw the spiritual senses from the literal sense of entering the real, historical world of the Bible (see *CCC*, 116–117).

Note: * Hesitant to write in your Bible? For more flexibility (and space), try sticky notes instead! If you wish, you can later transfer them to a notebook to provide an ongoing journal of your insights.

- The third prompt (identified/symbolized by 🕯) helps you to make what you've read *your own* by "confronting" the scripture passage with yourself. This expression of prayer is called *meditation* (see *CCC*, 2705–2706).*

    Meditating on the scriptures "engages thought, imagination, emotion, and desire" and leads us to the ultimate goal of "the knowledge of the love of the Lord Jesus, to union with him" (*CCC*, 2708). This third prompt is the most personal of the three; if praying in a group, you might choose to simply write down your thoughts rather than share them with the group.

Closing Prayer

Adapted from the Collect prayer of the following Sunday's Mass (the prayer right before the first reading), the closing prayer embodies the spirit of "Let us pray," as it reminds each of us that in prayer, we are truly with Christ, and that with his Body, we are never alone.

Each closing prayer in this book repeats for the week, leading up to the Sunday where the Collect prayer that inspired it is proclaimed at Mass. This enables you to grow familiar with the liturgical season's themes and the Church's vocabulary of prayer. As you hear similar words at a Saturday Vigil or Sunday Mass, allow your own prayers to be truly united, in Jesus Christ, with those of his entire Body—across all time and places—yearning toward greater, more perfect love *in* and *through* him.

Practical Tips

If you're praying with more than one person, allow one person to read the prayer aloud and have all others reply **Amen**.

If you would like to see the full Collect prayer for a particular week of the liturgical year, search online (the information is available for free on many websites) or look in a missal.

Note: * Meditation, vocal prayer, and contemplation are the three expressions of prayer the Church encourages in our prayer lives.

Lent: Gospel of Mark

Starting Simply

The Gospel of Mark is the shortest of the four gospels and moves in a vivid, action-packed style with a significant emphasis (six out of sixteen chapters!) on the events of the week leading up to Jesus's death and Resurrection. This shorter length and focus make it ideal for reading in full during the season of Lent.

While details of Mark's personal identity are not known for certain, his writing reveals that he spoke both Aramaic and Greek, and his gospel is widely thought to have been written between AD 50 and 70. Some early historical traditions suggest a connection between the gospel writer and the person (or people) named Mark found elsewhere in scripture (see Col 4:10, Phlm 1:24, 2 Tm 4:11, and 1 Pt 5:13, as well as John Mark in Acts 12:12 and 15:37). Mark could also be the unnamed "young man" mentioned in Mark 14:51–52.

Mark's inspired words show that if we simply have faith, Jesus will respond to our prayerful conversations with him.

Ash Wednesday

Morning Prayer

Psalm Verse

> Happy is he whose help is in the God of Jacob, **whose hope is in the LORD his God.**
>
> —Psalm 146:5

Contemplate

God is already helping you, carrying you, guiding you. Allow yourself to embrace the quiet, interior happiness we find in God's presence.

God, you are the creator of all things, and I can trust in you, hope in you, and experience happiness knowing that you have brought me this far and have a plan for my future.

Enter the Word of God

Introduction

In first-century Greco-Roman culture, a *gospel* (meaning "good news") was a royal proclamation of great significance, such as victory in a military battle or the birth of a new king. Mark the evangelist* reveals Jesus right away, in his first sentence, as the *Christ* (or *Messiah* in Hebrew), which means the one anointed and chosen by God (see *CCC*, 436).

✳ Scripture Reading: Mark 1:1–15 ✳

Note: * *Evangelist* is the term for the inspired, human author of one of the gospel books of the Bible. By calling the scriptures "inspired," we mean that God acted in and through real human beings, making "use of their power and abilities" (see *CCC*, 105–108, and *Dei Verbum*, 11).

Evening Prayer

Verse to Remember

Repent and believe in the Good News. **The kingdom of God is at hand.**

—cf. Mark 1:15

Respond to God's Word

 Find John's major announcement.*

✝ Why do you think God wanted Jesus to go into the wilderness to be baptized, before being driven by the Holy Spirit farther away, alone?

Meditate: Repent in Hebrew comes from the word for "turn" and, in Greek, from the word for "a change of mind or thinking." In what way—big or small, visible or hidden—might the Holy Spirit be leading you to repent?

Closing Prayer

Let us pray: Almighty God, grant that we may grow in understanding of the riches hidden in Christ. Through Jesus Christ, Our Lord. **Amen.**

Thursday after Ash Wednesday

Morning Prayer

Psalm Verse

I meditate on all that you have done; . . . **I stretch out my hands to you.**

—Psalm 143:5b–6a

Note: * Consider underlining or highlighting in your Bible particular verses or details referenced in these prompts.

Contemplate

God gazes lovingly upon you as you remember all he has done for you.

Lord Jesus, I stretch out my heart to you, asking you to bring stillness and silence to my fears and worries so that I can see with amazement the good you have done in my life.

Enter the Word of God

Introduction

Mark tells the story of Jesus with a fast pace. His frequent use of the word *immediately* shows us the urgency and radical new kingdom Jesus is bringing. Simon, Andrew, James, and John respond in kind—*immediately* following Jesus as he goes on to teach in synagogues, just as other Jewish teachers (called *rabbis*) did.

✠ Scripture Reading: Mark 1:12–28* ✠

Evening Prayer

Verse to Remember

> Repent and believe in the Good News. **The kingdom of God is at hand.**
>
> —cf. Mark 1:15

Note: * Unclean spirits (also known as demons) are invisible, spiritual beings who freely refuse to follow God's plan (see CCC, 414). Demons cause harm to people; therefore, Jesus desires to free people from their domination (see CCC, 550). In the ancient world, people often associated what could have been symptoms of mental illness with the influence of "unclean spirits" or "demons." Due to advances in our understanding of psychological illness, the Church emphasizes the importance of differentiating between demonic oppression in a person (protection from this is called an *exorcism*) and a mental illness (CCC, 1673). Other mentions of unclean spirits in Mark include 5:2–13, 7:25, and 9:17–27.

Respond to God's Word

 Find the first command Jesus gives to the unclean spirit.

 What do you think Jesus means in verse 15: that time has been "fulfilled" or that it's the time of "fulfillment"?

 Meditate: Talk to or listen to God about what astounds or amazes you about him.

Closing Prayer

Let us pray: Almighty God, grant that we may grow in understanding of the riches hidden in Christ. Through Jesus Christ, Our Lord. **Amen.**

Friday after Ash Wednesday

Morning Prayer

Psalm Verse

> Create in me a clean heart, O God, **and put a new and right spirit within me.**
>
> —Psalm 51:10

Contemplate

God's Spirit, who is holy and living, gives you life and renews your life. Open yourself to the rejuvenation the Spirit wants to work in you today.

Holy Spirit, I seek you and long for the renewal you give. Take and transform all of my works, words, and service today. Lift me up in new ways.

Enter the Word of God

Introduction

The kingdom continues to spread at an urgent pace, yet Jesus still takes time to be attentive and responsive to those around him. Crowds of people are hearing about Jesus and coming to him, some from long distances away, to be healed of sickness in their bodies or set free from unclean, evil spirits who hurt them spiritually. Even Simon's mother-in-law is healed!*

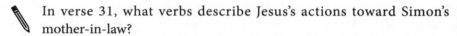

✶ Scripture Reading: Mark 1:29–38 ✶

Evening Prayer

Verse to Remember

> Repent and believe in the Good News. **The kingdom of God is at hand.**
>
> —cf. Mark 1:15

Respond to God's Word

In verse 31, what verbs describe Jesus's actions toward Simon's mother-in-law?

What do you think Jesus might have prayed about at this time of his ministry? See verse 35.

Meditate: What do you most need to pray about in a "lonely" or "deserted" place? Share it with God as best you can, silently, right now.

Closing Prayer

Let us pray: Almighty God, grant that we may grow in understanding of the riches hidden in Christ. Through Jesus Christ, Our Lord. **Amen.**

Note: * The wife of Simon (also called Peter and Cephas) is mentioned in 1 Corinthians 9:5. Choosing priests, and by extension bishops, who practice celibacy and do not marry is a practice (or discipline) of the Latin (Western) Rite of the Catholic Church (see CCC, 1579, 1599). Eastern Rite Catholics have a different practice of choosing among married men to ordain as priests (see CCC, 1580).

Saturday after Ash Wednesday

Morning Prayer

Psalm Verse

> For you, O LORD, have made me glad by your work; **at the works of your hands I sing for joy.**
>
> —Psalm 92:4

Contemplate

Imagine yourself being held securely by a God who, like a perfect parent, wants to give you good things, wants to bring you joy.

Lord, clear away my anxieties, my reservations, and my doubts so that I can remember the times you have made me glad and know that you desire good things for me.

Enter the Word of God

Introduction

Jesus is traveling from village to village throughout the region of Galilee, teaching in many Jewish synagogues, with his disciples following him. A man with leprosy* takes the initiative to come to Jesus, this rabbi (teacher) of growing fame. In Jesus's time, people with leprosy were excluded from daily life, especially the religious community, due to the belief that the medical condition made one religiously "impure."

✳ Scripture Reading: Mark 1:39–2:5 ✳

Note: *Leprosy (also known as Hansen's disease) is caused by a bacterial infection. In our modern world, it is curable and not highly contagious. In the first century, leprosy was incurable and contagious, and caused extreme suffering. Excluded from society, people with leprosy were often poor and ashamed—even though in John 9:2–3 Jesus explicitly teaches that physical illness or disability is not a consequence of individual or family sin.

Evening Prayer

Verse to Remember

> Repent and believe in the Good News. **The kingdom of God
> is at hand.**
>
> —cf. Mark 1:15

Respond to God's Word

 In verse 41, what verbs describe Jesus's actions toward the man with leprosy?

 How did the man with leprosy react to Jesus's healing and directions? How might he have felt?

 Meditate: What event, "matter," or "news" from your life do you (or might you in the future) share with others or offer God thanksgiving for?

Closing Prayer

Let us pray: Almighty God, grant that we may grow in understanding of the riches hidden in Christ. Through Jesus Christ, Our Lord. **Amen.**

First Sunday of Lent

Morning Prayer

Psalm Verse

> So I have looked upon you in the sanctuary, beholding your
> power and glory. **Because your merciful love is better than
> life.**
>
> —Psalm 63:2–3a

Contemplate

When you gaze upon God in a sanctuary, maybe a noisy church or maybe a quiet place, imagine God gazing back at you. Allow God's gaze to warm your soul.

God, you see me better than any person; you know my weaknesses and faults, and also my desires and good intentions. Bring me closer to you and the loving warmth of your mercy.

Enter the Word of God

Introduction

Jesus is back in his hometown. His ability to teach and to heal both physical and spiritual illness reveals his divine authority, leading some people to give glory to God and follow him to hear more teaching. Others criticize Jesus for claiming to forgive sins and for sharing meals with people known for their sinful behaviors. In verse 10, we first hear Jesus call himself the "Son of man,"* a title that emphasizes his humanity. Jesus is both fully God and fully human— just like us in everything but sin (see Heb 4:15).

✳ Scripture Reading: Mark 2:1–17 ✳

Evening Prayer

Verse to Remember

Create in me a clean heart, O God, **and put a new and right spirit within me.**

—Psalm 51:10

Note: * Jesus also often uses the title "Son of man" for himself in reference to his future Passion and death on the Cross. The phrase is first seen in the Bible in Daniel 7:9–14 as a vision of Jesus coming in glory, which we pray in the Creed at Mass: "He will come again in glory to judge the living and the dead and his kingdom will have no end."

Respond to God's Word

 What are the first words Jesus says to the man who is paralyzed?*

✝ Why do you think some scribes and Pharisees† keep following, watching, listening to, and talking about Jesus?

🕯 *Meditate:* How is Jesus speaking to you by name, even in your weaknesses, sins, disappointments, or failures?

Closing Prayer

Let us pray: Almighty God, grant that we may grow in understanding of the riches hidden in Christ. Through Jesus Christ, Our Lord. **Amen.**

First Monday of Lent

Morning Prayer

Psalm Verse

> For you bless the righteous, O Lord; **you cover him with favor as with a shield.**
>
> —Psalm 5:12

Notes: * The gospels mention people with many different disabilities—deafness, blindness, speech impediments, mobility restrictions, limb differences—as well as stories of people with mental health conditions and chronic illnesses. Biblical terms used to describe those with such disabilities (*lame, crippled, dumb,* and *demoniac*) capture a first-century mindset of seeing the disability and not the full human dignity of the disabled person.

† The Pharisees were one of many groups, or sects, within first-century Judaism. The Pharisees wanted to motivate other Jews to follow the Torah (also known as the Pentateuch, the Law of Moses, or the first five books of the Bible) more strictly. They were passionate about the scriptures and often questioned, debated, and argued with Jesus about his teachings. Some Pharisees opposed Jesus, while other Pharisees became his disciples and even apostles.

Contemplate

Visualize being completely covered and surrounded by God's shield, how safe divine protection is, what a refuge it is.

God, you are my shield, my protector, my refuge. Give me relief from the criticism of others, my doubts of my own worth, and the earthly challenges I face today.

Enter the Word of God

Introduction

The gospel announcement that Jesus, the Son of God, has arrived is exciting good news, like a wedding. In the first century, weddings were large celebrations (in stark contrast to the restraint of a fast*) involving the entire community and extended families. Family networks were especially significant in the ancient world because they shared wealth, food, and shelter, and provided physical protection to one another.

✳ Scripture Reading: Mark 2:18–3:6† ✳

Evening Prayer

Verse to Remember

> Create in me a clean heart, O God, **and put a new and right spirit within me.**
>
> —Psalm 51:10

Notes: * 2:18—To fast is to freely choose to not do or have something that one enjoys. Today, people freely choose to fast before receiving the Body of Christ in Communion (see *CCC*, 1387) and to prepare for liturgical celebrations, such as Easter (see *CCC*, 2043).

† The Sabbath is "a day to honor God" (*CCC*, 2173).

Respond to God's Word

 What jumps out at you in today's passage?

✝ How is Jesus's announcement and personal presence of the kingdom of God like a wedding?

🕯 *Meditate:* Open yourself to Jesus the bridegroom's presence in you. Ask Jesus to be with you for a particular reason, goal, or challenge.

Closing Prayer

Let us pray: God our Father, nourish us inwardly by your Word, that with spiritual sight made pure, we may rejoice to behold your glory. Through Jesus Christ, Our Lord. **Amen.**

First Tuesday of Lent

Morning Prayer

Psalm Verse

> Who shall ascend the hill [mountain] of the LORD? **And who shall stand in his holy place?**
>
> —Psalm 24:3

Contemplate

Listen for God calling you, inviting you by name to a quiet, holy mountaintop place of peace and friendship together with him.

God our Father, your holy place is eternal, infinite in love, peace, and goodness, which we glimpse merely shadows of in our earthly lives. I open my heart to you, to be lifted up into your holy place.

Enter the Word of God

Introduction

Jesus leaves the small city of Capernaum and heads toward the Sea of Galilee, where people from both Jewish and gentile regions are coming to experience his itinerant ministry. Before returning home, Jesus goes up a small mountain, where he calls twelve* ordinary men to be with him and appoints them to share in his ministry of announcing the kingdom of God in word and deed (see *CCC*, 542).

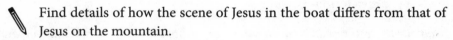 ✳ Scripture Reading: Mark 3:7–20 ✳

Evening Prayer

Verse to Remember

> Create in me a clean heart, O God, **and put a new and right spirit within me.**
>
> —Psalm 51:10

Respond to God's Word

Find details of how the scene of Jesus in the boat differs from that of Jesus on the mountain.

What does it mean for us, as present-day disciples, that Jesus sent twelve seemingly ordinary men out to do God's work?

Meditate: The first action of the Twelve, before going out to preach or heal others, is to be with Jesus. How is Jesus calling you to be with him?

Closing Prayer

Let us pray: God our Father, nourish us inwardly by your Word, that with spiritual sight made pure, we may rejoice to behold your glory. Through Jesus Christ, Our Lord. **Amen.**

Note: * The most specific and precise term for these men used in the Bible is the Twelve. They are also understood as and called disciples and apostles. See diagram on page 160 to visualize how these three terms are used to describe Jesus's followers.

First Wednesday of Lent

Morning Prayer

Psalm Verse

> [The Lord] subdued peoples under us, and nations under our feet. **He chose our heritage for us, the pride [glory] of Jacob whom he loves.**
>
> —Psalm 47:3–4

Contemplate

Our only true enemy is the Evil One, who wants to divide, discourage, and ultimately destroy us. God has defeated Evil, yet he trusts us to wait as his full and final plan unfolds. Take comfort in knowing that you are protected and loved by this victorious God.

God our Protector and Comforter, give me the hope and confidence that you are with us, even in times of darkness. I pray that your victory would be seen more and more in the world around us.

Enter the Word of God

Introduction

As Jesus's reputation continues to spread, his relatives (many cousins, "brethren," and other kin, all connected by bonds of genealogy and marriage) are concerned about him. Their concerns are not unfounded, as we see religious scholars make the journey north from Jerusalem to accuse Jesus of being possessed by Beelzebul, one of many names for the Evil One.* Jesus responds with his own teaching about who God is and how God is at work.

✳ Scripture Reading: Mark 3:20–30 ✳

Note: * The Evil One is also called Satan, the devil, the Adversary, and the Accuser.

Evening Prayer

Verse to Remember

> Create in me a clean heart, O God, **and put a new and right spirit within me.**
>
> —Psalm 51:10

Respond to God's Word

 What is Jesus's rhetorical, logical point in saying, "How can Satan cast out Satan?"

✝ Jesus states his game plan, that he is going to take the personification of evil captive and rescue everything and everyone who had been trapped. What does this reveal to us about Jesus?

Meditate: To blaspheme is to deny or disregard God's true identity. If someone rejects God's love poured out in the Holy Spirit, then that person is not open to receiving the mercy and forgiveness God wants to extend (*CCC*, 734). No sin is too large for God's forgiveness. Silently reflect on a sin that you once felt (or do feel) ashamed or concerned about. Thank Jesus for forgiving your sin and placing you in his family as a brother or sister.

Closing Prayer

Let us pray: God our Father, nourish us inwardly by your Word, that with spiritual sight made pure, we may rejoice to behold your glory. Through Jesus Christ, Our Lord. **Amen.**

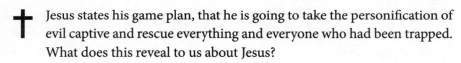

First Thursday of Lent

Morning Prayer

Psalm Verse

> My heart is steadfast, O God, **my heart is steadfast!**
>
> —Psalm 57:7

Contemplate

Imagine God looking at you, your heart steadfast, ready, and devoted to him.

Jesus, you welcome me into your Body, your family. Make me steadfastly devoted to being near you and listening to you.

Enter the Word of God

Introduction

Jesus's relatives arrive at the house where Jesus is inside, responding to the religious experts who had made the trip from Jerusalem to confront him. Jesus continues to reveal through these examples that being his disciple (follower) is not predetermined by one's religious or cultural background, or even one's family or geographic origin. Instead, it is a choice to respond to God that is open to all (see *CCC*, 543).

✵ Scripture Reading: Mark 3:31–35 ✵

Evening Prayer

Verse to Remember

> Create in me a clean heart, O God, **and put a new and right spirit within me.**
>
> —Psalm 51:10

Respond to God's Word

 Why is Jesus's family concerned about him?

✝ By sharing in Jesus's baptism, we become his brothers and sisters. What does calling Jesus your "brother" reveal to you about who he truly is?

🕯 *Meditate:* How is Jesus challenging you to see the Church, family, and your relationships with others as he does?

Closing Prayer

Let us pray: God our Father, nourish us inwardly by your Word, that with spiritual sight made pure, we may rejoice to behold your glory. Through Jesus Christ, Our Lord. **Amen.**

First Friday of Lent

Morning Prayer

Psalm Verse

> O Lord, open my lips, **and my mouth shall show forth your praise.**
>
> —Psalm 51:15

Contemplate

Consider the trust God places in you, that he uses your words for his praise and glory.

Come, Holy Spirit, guide my mind and lips that I may understand and speak your words of comfort, truth, and love to those around me.

Enter the Word of God

Introduction

Jesus begins teaching a large crowd from a boat on the Sea of Galilee. Afterward, the Twelve and some other close disciples ask Jesus to interpret the parables for them. While Jesus was neither the first nor the only rabbi (teacher) in the ancient world to use parables, these stories and sayings with a shocking twist were a distinctive and pivotal element of his teaching (see *CCC*, 546). Parables invite us to enter into open-ended pondering of the ways the kingdom of God is both similar to and strangely different from the reality we have grown accustomed to in our human experiences.

✳ Scripture Reading: Mark 4:1–36 ✳

Evening Prayer

Verse to Remember

> Create in me a clean heart, O God, **and put a new and right spirit within me.**
>
> —Psalm 51:10

Respond to God's Word

 What do Jesus's words reveal about the difference in how his followers ("disciples") receive his parables, compared to the crowds in general?

 What do these parables reveal about the kingdom of God, now and in eternity?

 Meditate: What has the Holy Spirit revealed to you in a personal way? Offer thanksgiving for this, or ask the Lord for more insight into something you are seeking to understand more deeply.

Closing Prayer

Let us pray: God our Father, nourish us inwardly by your Word, that with spiritual sight made pure, we may rejoice to behold your glory. Through Jesus Christ, Our Lord. **Amen.**

First Saturday of Lent

Morning Prayer

Psalm Verse

> I rise before dawn and cry for help; **I hope in your words.**
>
> —Psalm 119:147

Contemplate

God sees your faith and is moved with compassion. Rest a moment in being known by God, knowing that he cares about you.

Lord, give me the confidence to place my hope in you and receive the peace that only you give.

Enter the Word of God

Introduction

That evening, after Jesus has finished teaching, he and the disciples set out to cross the Sea of Galilee. Due to rough winds, the boat begins to take on water from waves, causing the men to wonder if Jesus even cares about what is happening. This leads to an opportunity for Jesus to reveal who he is from an unexpected perspective.

✴ Scripture Reading: Mark 4:35–41 ✴

Evening Prayer

Verse to Remember

> Create in me a clean heart, O God, **and put a new and right spirit within me.**
>
> —Psalm 51:10

Respond to God's Word

 What is the main concern of those who awaken Jesus on the boat?

✝ Jesus says a similar thing to the stormy weather that he said earlier to an evil spirit: "Peace. Be still" (4:39; see also 1:25). Why might Jesus emphasize these commands?

Meditate: Share thanksgiving for a time Jesus spoke peace into your life, or ask for divine peace or stillness in a place where you need it right now.

Closing Prayer

Let us pray: God our Father, nourish us inwardly by your Word, that with spiritual sight made pure, we may rejoice to behold your glory. Through Jesus Christ, Our Lord. **Amen.**

Second Sunday of Lent

Morning Prayer

Psalm Verse

> I thank you that you have answered me **and have become my salvation.**
>
> —Psalm 118:21

Contemplate

Unite your heart and soul to Jesus in pure faith that Jesus is your rescuer, your Savior—no matter who you are, where you live, or what your life is like.

Jesus, you don't choose to enter into my life because I am perfect or even good, or because I "act" like a religious person. You rescue and save me because you see my faith and hope in you. I praise you as my Savior.

Enter the Word of God

Introduction

Jesus and his disciples have crossed the Sea of Galilee and are now on the eastern side in an area called the Decapolis, a region with a predominantly Greek, gentile* population. Jesus demonstrates that his divine authority is not limited by geographic or ethnic boundaries as he engages in a personal encounter with a gentile man involving a herd of pigs, an animal Jews were to avoid (see Dt 14:8).

✠ Scripture Reading: Mark 5:1–20 ✠

Note: * From the Jewish perspective, all people who were not Jews were called *Gentiles* or the/all/other "nations." *Greek* is both the term for the official language of the Roman Empire in Jesus's time and a term to describe an ethnicity.

Evening Prayer

Verse to Remember

> God himself will set me free, **from the hunter's snare.**
>
> —cf. Psalm 91:3

Respond to God's Word

 What jumps out at you today in this passage?

Jesus meets a man with an unclean spirit, who is not Jewish, as Jesus and his disciples are. What is the man's first response to Jesus? What do you think he expected of Jesus?

Meditate: The man who had the unclean spirit asks to start following Jesus too. What do you notice in Jesus's answer to him? Prayerfully reflect on a time you may have felt like this man in your relationship of prayer with God.

Closing Prayer

Let us pray: God our Father, nourish us inwardly by your Word, that with spiritual sight made pure, we may rejoice to behold your glory. Through Jesus Christ, Our Lord. **Amen.**

Second Monday of Lent

Morning Prayer

Psalm Verse

> Deep calls to deep in the roar of your torrents, **and all your waves and breakers sweep over me.**
>
> —Psalm 42:8, NABRE

Contemplate

Imagine God with you, speaking to you, in the deep waters of chaos and uncertainty.

Jesus, you are Emmanuel, "God with us." Remind me of this in times of struggle or suffering.

Enter the Word of God

Introduction

Jesus has left the gentile Decapolis area and returned to the western side of the Sea of Galilee. Here he is speaking to a Jewish synagogue leader, someone of significance and influence, when, in sharp contrast, a woman—someone of no real importance who has been excluded from community religious practices due to her medical condition—interrupts the conversation.

 Scripture Reading: Mark 5:21–43

Evening Prayer

Verse to Remember

> God himself will set me free, **from the hunter's snare.**
>
> —cf. Psalm 91:3

Respond to God's Word

What do you think the woman believes would happen when she touches Jesus's clothes?

What do we learn about Jesus's character from how he relates both to Jairus and his family and to the woman in the crowd?

 Meditate: Without any barriers or worries about who you are or how you might appear, reach out to Jesus in prayer with something important to you.

Closing Prayer

Let us pray: God, author of every mercy and of all goodness, look graciously on us, that we may always be lifted up by your mercy. Through Jesus Christ, Our Lord. **Amen.**

Second Tuesday of Lent

Morning Prayer

Psalm Verse

> Vindicate me, O God, and defend my cause against an ungod-
> ly people; **from deceitful and unjust men deliver me!**
> —Psalm 43:1

Contemplate

Consider our God, who is a rescuer, who delivers and relieves us from situations out of our control in unexpected ways.

*Lord Jesus, because you became human, you truly understand the division and
tensions that arise between people. Forgive the wrongs I have done to others and
protect me from harm in my relationships with others.*

Enter the Word of God

Introduction

Jesus heads south to Nazareth and, despite teaching in a synagogue, is surprised
by the lack of faith of his fellow Jews in this area. Undismayed, Jesus continues
teaching and again sends out the Twelve to announce the kingdom of God in
word and deed. Before telling us of their return, Mark includes a disturbing
interlude account of how in the recent past King Herod imprisoned and then
killed John the Baptist.

✳ Scripture Reading: Mark 6:1–31 ✳

Evening Prayer

Verse to Remember

> God himself will set me free, **from the hunter's snare.**
> —cf. Psalm 91:3

Respond to God's Word

 What do you notice in this passage today?

✝ How might Jesus's disciples feel when they first hear this news about John the Baptist? Could it change their understanding of Jesus and his mission?

Meditate: This story about the death of John the Baptist is the longest segment in Mark's gospel where Jesus is absent from the scene. Pray for a situation involving yourself or others where you want to see Jesus's presence more clearly.

Closing Prayer

Let us pray: God, author of every mercy and of all goodness, look graciously on us, that we may always be lifted up by your mercy. Through Jesus Christ, Our Lord. **Amen.**

Second Wednesday of Lent

Morning Prayer

Psalm Verse

You led your people like a flock **by the hand of Moses and Aaron.**

—Psalm 77:20

Contemplate

Place yourself in God's loving care, knowing that you are a sheep in his flock and he wants you to have the guidance of a Good Shepherd.

God our Father, you have led us, your people who tend to wander like sheep, with love and compassion going back thousands of years. Fill me with the comfort and protection of knowing you are my shepherd today.

Enter the Word of God

Introduction

Jesus tells the Twelve he sent out to now come and rest, to be with him again as when Jesus first appointed them to this mission. A large crowd seemingly ruins the quiet retreat by following Jesus. Yet Jesus is compassionate and knows how much people need him. He shows no anger, and in fact reveals his depth of compassion for them because they lack a shepherd.

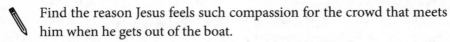

✳ Scripture Reading: Mark 6:30–44 ✳

Evening Prayer

Verse to Remember

> God himself will set me free, **from the hunter's snare.**
>
> —cf. Psalm 91:3

Respond to God's Word

Find the reason Jesus feels such compassion for the crowd that meets him when he gets out of the boat.

Jesus's instruction for the thousands of people to sit in groups of hundreds and fifties resembles how God's people, Israel, stopped for breaks while journeying to the Promised Land. What is Jesus showing about his true identity?

Meditate: Jesus's first reaction to the crowd's hunger is to ask his disciples to do something about it. Why do you think Jesus does this? Recall in prayer a time when Jesus challenged you, and what ended up happening.

Closing Prayer

Let us pray: God, author of every mercy and of all goodness, look graciously upon us, that we may always be lifted up by your mercy. Through Jesus Christ, Our Lord. **Amen.**

Second Thursday of Lent

Morning Prayer

Psalm Verse

> O shepherd of Israel, hear us, **shine forth from your cheru-**
> **bim throne.**
> —Psalm 80:1–2, Liturgy of the Hours translation

Contemplate

As you pause to listen to God, imagine God's delight in your attentiveness.

Lord our Shepherd, help me see your light shining and know your constant care in times of distress.

Enter the Word of God

Introduction

Jesus continues to include the Twelve in the announcement that God's kingdom has arrived in a new and definitive way by engaging them as actors in this miracle of the feeding of the five thousand, the first of two "feeding" miracles in Mark's gospel. Afterward, the Twelve head off by boat to Bethsaida, apart from Jesus. Just as Jesus had compassion on the crowds, he has compassion on his fearful followers, who seem not to fully understand the events of the day.

 Scripture Reading: Mark 6:39–52

Evening Prayer

Verse to Remember

> God himself will set me free, **from the hunter's snare.**
> —cf. Psalm 91:3

Respond to God's Word

 What makes Jesus change his plan as he walks across the water at night?

 Mark connects the disciples' astonishment with their lack of understanding about what Jesus did with the loaves. What are they missing?

 Meditate: Ask Jesus to visit you, to walk to you in a situation that is out of your control.

Closing Prayer

Let us pray: God, author of every mercy and of all goodness, look graciously on us, that we may always be lifted up by your mercy. Through Jesus Christ, Our Lord. **Amen.**

Second Friday of Lent

Morning Prayer

Psalm Verse

> Purge me with hyssop, and I shall be clean; **wash me, and I shall be whiter than snow.**
>
> —Psalm 51:7

Contemplate

Allow the purification of God to wash over you: his gentleness and desire to make you reflect his goodness in the world.

Jesus, I am thankful that you are truly my advocate who wants to inflame my heart with love. Fill me more and more with your purity of heart.

Enter the Word of God

Introduction

Such contrasts! Some people have no confusion about who Jesus is and eagerly come to him for healing, while others follow Jesus to critically question him and challenge his teachings. The Pharisees and scribes are Jewish religious leaders who want more ordinary Jews to follow the ritual rules of the Torah,* including those that pertain to eating. Jesus calls them hypocrites for not loving God in their hearts but acting as if they honor God on the outside. These Jewish religious leaders are persistent and keep arguing with Jesus about following their ritual rules for spiritual purity.

✳ Scripture Reading: Mark 6:53–7:23 ✳

Evening Prayer

Verse to Remember

God himself will set me free, **from the hunter's snare.**
—cf. Psalm 91:3

Respond to God's Word

 What jumps out at you in today's reading?

✝ How were the human traditions from the Jewish elders of the time misleading people when it came to understanding God's plan of salvation?

Meditate: Jesus demonstrates that adhering externally to human-made rules is not what sets God's family apart or makes it holy. In prayer, share with God how you feel about being part of his family because of your relationship of the heart with him, and not due to external rules or customs.

Closing Prayer

Let us pray: God, author of every mercy and of all goodness, look graciously on us, that we may always be lifted up by your mercy. Through Jesus Christ, Our Lord. **Amen.**

Note: * The Torah (also the Pentateuch or the Law) is the first five books of the Old Testament.

Second Saturday of Lent

Morning Prayer

Psalm Verse

You have exalted my horn like that of the wild ox; **you have poured over me fresh oil.**

—Psalm 92:10

Contemplate

Imagine God exalting and delighting in what makes you uniquely you.

Lord God, give me a fresh anointing as with oil to persevere in prayer with new vigor.

Enter the Word of God

Introduction

Jesus leaves the place of debate with Jewish leaders and goes to the far northwestern cities of Tyre and Sidon, where he enters the house of a ritually "unclean" gentile woman, thereby making himself ritually unclean (according to the Torah). The woman asks for the same bread God gave his Chosen People, Israel. Declaring her faith in Jesus, she is the first person in Mark's gospel to use the title "Lord" (see *CCC*, 446–451). Next, Jesus returns to the Decapolis, where the gentile disciple whom he had instructed to share what Jesus had done for him (5:20) had apparently been quite successful!

✠ Scripture Reading: Mark 7:24–37 ✠

Evening Prayer

Verse to Remember

God himself will set me free, **from the hunter's snare.**

—cf. Psalm 91:3

Respond to God's Word

 How is it possible that so many people, in places as far away and both ethnically and religiously diverse as Tyre, have heard about Jesus?

 What does Jesus see in the Syrophoenician woman's heart?

 Meditate: This woman is authentic and spontaneous in her conversation with Jesus. She doesn't hold back or speak to him only in formal or official language. Put the expectations of others or the pressures we place on ourselves to "sound good" aside today, and pray to Jesus in your own unique words.

Closing Prayer

Let us pray: God, author of every mercy and of all goodness, look graciously on us, that we may always be lifted up by your mercy. Through Jesus Christ, Our Lord. **Amen.**

Third Sunday of Lent

Morning Prayer

Psalm Verse

> Your decrees are very sure; holiness befits your house, O LORD, forevermore.
>
> —Psalm 93:5

Contemplate

Envision being at home with the Lord.

Father God, you have set aside your house for a special purpose. Your home is solid, sure, and secure. When I doubt and am confused, give me assurance that I am always at home in your house.

Enter the Word of God

Introduction

Mark leads us further into the "bread" theme, which began in chapter 6. No matter what their situation, people from all walks of life are hungry. Jesus shares in their humanity and has compassion on them; he wants to feed them with the bread only he can provide.* Yet ironically, as the Twelve head back across the Sea of Galilee with Jesus, they forget to bring enough bread for the trip!

✳ Scripture Reading: Mark 8:1–25 ✳

Evening Prayer

Verse to Remember

> May we live not by bread only, **but by every word falling from your lips.**
>
> —cf. Matthew 4:4

Respond to God's Word

 How does this crowd differ from the Pharisees?

 What does Jesus want the disciples to understand?

 Meditate: The disciples are a bit like the blind man in Bethsaida—coming to see things gradually. Reflect in prayer on how your relationship with Jesus has been like the gradual healing of this blind man or the disciples forgetting bread and misunderstanding what God was showing them.

Closing Prayer

Let us pray: God, author of every mercy and of all goodness, look graciously on us, that we may always be lifted up by your mercy. Through Jesus Christ, Our Lord. **Amen.**

Note: * Mark 8:6, where "having given thanks" is a form of the Greek verb *eucharisteo*, is a second foreshadowing (following 6:41) of the Last Supper and the Sacrament of the Eucharist.

Third Monday of Lent

Morning Prayer

Psalm Verse

> How lovely is your dwelling place, **O Lord of hosts!**
>
> —Psalm 84:1

Contemplate

Think about the love of a God who intentionally dwells with us, who makes his home not merely in the cosmic, heavenly places but on earth, traveling about with us.

Bless us, O Lord, as we follow you in our daily lives.

Enter the Word of God

Introduction

After the unique, gradual healing of a man who was blind, the Twelve experience their own gradual transformation, entering into God's plan and kingdom more deeply. In response to a question from Jesus, Simon Peter states clearly that Jesus is the "Christ," which means the Messiah, or God's special anointed or chosen one (see *CCC*, 436). Jesus follows up his teaching about the suffering to come in his future with an announcement that some of the people listening will live to see God's kingdom come in a new way.

✳ Scripture Reading: Mark 8:22–9:1 ✳

Evening Prayer

Verse to Remember

> May we live not by bread only, **but by every word falling from your lips.**
>
> —cf. Matthew 4:4

Respond to God's Word

 What do you notice in today's passage?

✝ At the end of this conversation, Jesus predicts that some will indeed see God's kingdom come into power in their lifetime. What do you think Jesus means?

🕯 *Meditate:* This is a new and challenging teaching for Jesus's followers. Ask the Lord in prayer what new thing he might be showing you at this time.

Closing Prayer

Let us pray: O God, who through your Word reconciles the human race to yourself in a wonderful way, open our hearts to your renewal in grace. Through Jesus Christ, Our Lord. **Amen.**

Third Tuesday of Lent

Morning Prayer

Psalm Verse

> May God be gracious to us and bless us **and make his face to shine upon us.**
>
> —Psalm 67:1

Contemplate

Embrace the glistening, dazzling, stunning brightness of God's face, revealed to you and shining on you right now.

God, allow your brightness and light to penetrate me so that I might reflect your light to others.

Enter the Word of God

Introduction

Six days after Jesus began to teach about his future rejection and death, Jesus takes Peter, James, and John up a mountain, where they experience an incredible theophany, a manifestation of God like those of the Old Testament (see *CCC*, 697, 707). This Transfiguration is both a glimpse of God's kingdom and a revelation of how Jesus connects to God's plan to reunite his family, which began with God giving the Israelites the Law (represented by Moses) and the Prophets (represented by Elijah; see *CCC*, 555).

✴ Scripture Reading: Mark 9:1–10 ✴

Evening Prayer

Verse to Remember

> May we live not by bread only, **but by every word falling from your lips.**
>
> —cf. Matthew 4:4

Respond to God's Word

How might Peter, James, and John have felt about this dramatic experience—and the perplexing instructions from Jesus that followed it?

This scene includes a rare revelation directly from God the Father. Why do you think God makes this revelation at this time?

Meditate: Have you ever experienced a mountaintop moment, when the presence of God was revealed to you in an unmistakable way? Recall that experience in prayer and allow it to strengthen you, or ask the Lord to give you a memorable experience and to reveal himself more plainly to you.

Closing Prayer

Let us pray: O God, who through your Word reconciles the human race to yourself in a wonderful way, open our hearts to your renewal in grace. Through Jesus Christ, Our Lord. **Amen.**

Third Wednesday of Lent

Morning Prayer

Psalm Verse

Give ear, O LORD, to my prayer; **listen to my cry of supplication.**

—Psalm 86:6

Contemplate

Imagine God listening to your heart, knowing you before you even speak or think a word.

Jesus, I believe in you. Hear and answer my greatest needs for this day.

Enter the Word of God

Introduction

Jesus, Peter, James, and John are discussing what has just happened as they walk back to the other disciples. Returning, they discover that the disciples who were left behind have been surrounded by a large crowd, and experts on the Torah (the Law) are arguing with them. Jesus is slow to anger and merciful both to his disciples and to people in the crowd as he teaches them that connecting to God in prayer, not their own skill or human authority, is what is most important.

✠ Scripture Reading: Mark 9:9–29 ✠

Evening Prayer

Verse to Remember

May we live not by bread only, **but by every word falling from your lips.**

—cf. Matthew 4:4

Respond to God's Word

 What would it be like to be part of the crowd, watching all of this unfold? What would stand out to you?

 How do the words exchanged between the boy's father and Jesus show us that Jesus answers prayers even of those with doubts and struggles?

 Meditate: Society (and sometimes even religious people) makes it seem as if we must be perfect for Jesus to want us as his followers. But this is not true. Believing that Jesus is truly who he says he is—the Messiah, the Son of God—allows Jesus to increase our trust in him from the inside. Pray as the boy's father does in this scene: declare your belief to Jesus, and ask him to help you in areas of doubt or confusion.

Closing Prayer

Let us pray: O God, who through your Word reconciles the human race to yourself in a wonderful way, open our hearts to your renewal in grace. Through Jesus Christ, Our Lord. **Amen.**

Third Thursday of Lent

Morning Prayer

Psalm Verse

> Mighty King, lover of justice, **you have established equity; you have executed justice.**
>
> —Psalm 99:4

Contemplate

God's kingdom is the person of Jesus the Messiah and the community of all who are joined to Christ's Body, and it is present within each person who believes in the Son of God.

Christ Jesus, you are all-powerful, yet you turned our ideas upside down by how you chose to die. Lead us deeper into the mysteries of your kingdom.

Enter the Word of God

Introduction

Jesus and his followers return to Capernaum for the final time in Mark's gospel. Jesus has continued to teach his disciples that he will rise from the dead, but they focus on debating among themselves about which of them is the greatest.

✳ Scripture Reading: Mark 9:28–37 ✳

Evening Prayer

Verse to Remember

> May we live not by bread only, **but by every word falling from your lips.**
>
> —cf. Matthew 4:4

Respond to God's Word

 What do you notice in today's passage?

 Why do you think the disciples are afraid to ask Jesus about his teaching?

Meditate: Jesus's disciples view themselves as in competition with one another for the status of being the most important, best, or most powerful. Jesus shows them that being better than others does not matter at all in the kingdom of God. Offer to Jesus a situation in your life where you need refreshment and renewal from the pressures of feeling better or worse than others.

Closing Prayer

Let us pray: O God, who through your Word reconciles the human race to yourself in a wonderful way, open our hearts to your renewal in grace. Through Jesus Christ, Our Lord. **Amen.**

Third Friday of Lent

Morning Prayer

Psalm Verse

> For I know my transgressions, **and my sin is ever before me.**
> —Psalm 51:3

Contemplate

The Son of God, truly human, experienced the full range of human emotions and temptations. When Jesus forgives, our sins are forgotten. Gaze on the Lord in that freedom and lightness of having your burdens, your sins, swept away.

Lord Jesus, heal me from the effects of my past sins; renew and restore me to live in your Spirit.

Enter the Word of God

Introduction

Jesus teaches that God's true family, those who bear his name as his "little ones," is wider and more diverse than the disciples anticipate. Because of this magnitude and breadth of the Church, believers will be tempted to make themselves seem greater than others or to lack concern for the spiritual well-being of others, even leading them to sin. Jesus concludes with an observation that both salt and fire are natural purifiers and preservatives essential to human life. Once they are gone, they are not easily replaced.

✷ Scripture Reading: Mark 9:38–50* ✷

Note: * "Gehenna" is a valley located on the southwest side of Jerusalem that was used in the first century for disposing dead animal carcasses. It symbolized the eternal destiny of those who reject God.

Evening Prayer

Verse to Remember

> May we live not by bread only, **but by every word falling from your lips.**
>
> —cf. Matthew 4:4

Respond to God's Word

 What error in thought and action do John and the other disciples make?

✝ Based on Jesus's teaching in this passage, how can we in the Body of Christ live at peace with one another?

Meditate: Salt is a unique substance. It purifies, preserves, and enhances flavor—and when it is missing, no other spice can take its place. In prayer, share with God a situation where you feel your salt is running low and needs to be refreshed.

Closing Prayer

Let us pray: O God, who through your Word reconciles the human race to yourself in a wonderful way, open our hearts to your renewal in grace. Through Jesus Christ, Our Lord. **Amen.**

Third Saturday of Lent

Morning Prayer

Psalm Verse

> Long have I known from your testimonies **that you have founded them for ever.**
>
> —Psalm 119:152

Contemplate

God, the Creator of the Universe, of all that exists, is outside of time, with a plan to fulfill all things in perfection and love, and this includes you!

God our Creator, grant me the gift of knowing that you are in control and allowing your eternal plan to unfold.

Enter the Word of God

Introduction

Jesus leaves Galilee and heads south to a new region, Judea. Crowds continue to flock to Jesus for his teaching, while the Pharisees want to test him on his interpretations of Torah Law. Jesus answers questions on the interpretation of one part of the scriptures by turning to Genesis, providing a fresh response to a hotly debated question concerning divorce by pointing to God's original, grand plan for the world, the peace and paradise of the Garden of Eden (see *CCC*, 111–114).

✳ Scripture Reading: Mark 10:1–16* ✳

Evening Prayer

Verse to Remember

> May we live not by bread only, **but by every word falling from your lips.**
>
> —cf. Matthew 4:4

Note: * Divorce was permitted in Judaism. Since only a husband could divorce a wife and a woman typically needed to remarry to avoid poverty, the institution of a bill, or certificate, of divorce protected divorced women by allowing them to legally remarry. Jesus explains that in God's original plan for humanity—glimpsed in the perfect peace and love of Adam and Eve before sin entered the world—divorce would never even be imagined because all people would live in perfect peace, without sin. Divorce brings harm to people, especially deserted spouses and children (see CCC, 2385). Sometimes civil divorce is the only possible way of ensuring protection, rights, and care of a spouse or children. In these cases, civil divorce itself is not a moral offense (see CCC, 2383). People who are divorced are not "automatically excommunicated"; they are still in full communion with the Church so long as they do not remarry without a decree of nullity.

Respond to God's Word

 Jesus's answer to the Pharisees references the Book of Genesis. Find the words and phrases from Genesis that you recognize in Jesus's answer.

✝ Jesus shows how God, knowing our weaknesses, guides his people as they grow in knowledge of him. What does this reveal about God's plan for all of creation?

Meditate: After Jesus's teaching, the disciples reprimand people from the crowd who draw close to Jesus with their children. Imagine the scene in prayer: Where do you find yourself? Are you a child being brought to Jesus? A parent receiving a reprimand? Misunderstanding Jesus and acting wrongly like the disciples? How is God calling you to take a step forward?

Closing Prayer

Let us pray: O God, who through your Word reconciles the human race to yourself in a wonderful way, open our hearts to your renewal in grace. Through Jesus Christ, Our Lord. **Amen.**

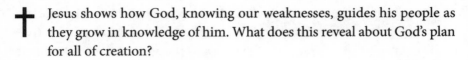

Fourth Sunday of Lent

Morning Prayer

Psalm Verse

Open to me the gates of righteousness, **that I may enter through them and give thanks to the LORD.**

—Psalm 118:19

Contemplate

It is not we who open the gate, but God.

Lord God, nourish my trust in you that with you all things are possible.

Enter the Word of God

Introduction

As Jesus heads toward Jerusalem, his interactions continue to reveal different aspects of what it means to be a disciple. Jesus teaches that we cannot save ourselves by our own efforts, achievements, religious behaviors, or virtues. Only God's plan of salvation, sending Jesus as the Messiah to give his life for us, makes it possible for us to be healed of sin and separation from God, welcomed into God's merciful arms, and slowly transformed and restored into God's image (see *CCC*, 1023–1029).

✳ Scripture Reading: Mark 10:17–34 ✳

Evening Prayer

Verse to Remember

> Jesus, Son of David, **have mercy on me!**
>
> —Mark 10:47

Respond to God's Word

 How does the Bible say that the disciples react to Jesus's answer to the rich man?

 Why is it impossible for us as mortal human beings to save ourselves?

Meditate: As you pray, set aside the accomplishments and virtues you are not relying on for salvation and give yourself over to Jesus as his follower. Feel the lifting of the burden of trying to do it yourself, and take comfort in knowing that God has an eternal plan for you in the world to come.

Closing Prayer

Let us pray: O God, who through your Word reconciles the human race to yourself in a wonderful way, open our hearts to your renewal in grace. Through Jesus Christ, Our Lord. **Amen.**

Fourth Monday of Lent

Morning Prayer

Psalm Verse

> L O R D, you have been our dwelling place **in all generations.**
>
> —Psalm 90:1

Contemplate

Enter into God's fullness as your dwelling place, his kingdom in this world and eternity.

God, you are our protection. Guide and correct my good intentions so that I can glorify you in all that I do.

Enter the Word of God

Introduction

Brothers James and John ask Jesus for a place of honor in his kingdom to come. Jesus's answer reveals both present and future truths, which will become clearer at Jesus's death and Resurrection. One example is the fullest meaning of baptism. Jesus calls the cup that he will drink his baptism, a revelation that his death will bring new life and that by joining ourselves to Christ Jesus in baptism, we will also follow him in resurrection (see *CCC*, 1010).

✳ Scripture Reading: Mark 10:32–45 ✳

Evening Prayer

Verse to Remember

> Jesus, Son of David, **have mercy on me!**
>
> —Mark 10:47

Respond to God's Word

 What is a ransom? How does paying a ransom work?

How is the glory that James and John are thinking of different from what Jesus is speaking of?

Meditate: Jesus came not to receive honor and earthly praises but to be a sacrifice for others, including you! Meditate on the dignity and worth God must see in you for God to ransom his only Son so that you may experience eternal life.

Closing Prayer

Let us pray: Lord God, help us follow the example of your Son, who handed himself over to death out of love for us and the whole world. Through Jesus Christ, Our Lord. **Amen.**

Fourth Tuesday of Lent

Morning Prayer

Psalm Verse

> LORD, what is man that you take notice of him; **the son of man, that you think of him?**
>
> —Psalm 144:3; NABRE

Contemplate

The Lord God is turning to you, interested in all that you think, do, and worry about, because he loves you.

Lord Jesus, hear me and help me when I call out to you in my heart today.

Enter the Word of God

Introduction

As Jesus is leaving Jericho, a sizable city closer to Jerusalem, he is interrupted by Bartimaeus and changes his plans to show mercy. Bartimaeus embodies the major themes of Mark's gospel as he boldly places his faith in Jesus, regardless of how he might appear to others, and receives new life and encouragement to continue following Jesus.

✳ Scripture Reading: Mark 10:46–52 ✳

Evening Prayer

Verse to Remember

> Jesus, Son of David, **have mercy on me!**
>
> —Mark 10:47

Respond to God's Word

 Why do you think some people try to make Bartimaeus quiet down?

✝ Bartimaeus's words are known as the Jesus Prayer. How do they sum up, in a concise way, God's plan of salvation?

Meditate: Pray Bartimaeus's words yourself, paying attention to what new blessing Jesus wants to give to you.

Closing Prayer

Let us pray: Lord God, help us follow the example of your Son, who handed himself over to death out of love for us and the whole world. Through Jesus Christ, Our Lord. **Amen.**

Fourth Wednesday of Lent

Morning Prayer

Psalm Verse

> It is the LORD who keeps faith for ever, **who is just to those who are oppressed.**
>   —Psalm 146:7, Liturgy of the Hours translation

Contemplate

Visualize God on the move, coming to you, loving you, ever faithful.

Son of God, you come toward us wherever we are, even in difficult situations and places where we feel captive. Thank you for being Emmanuel, God with us.

Enter the Word of God

Introduction

Jesus and the Twelve arrive in Jerusalem, and Jesus goes first to the Temple to look around before spending the night outside of the city, in Bethany. The next day, Jesus heads back to the Temple to teach and to remove those who were putting up barriers (such as selling overpriced animals for sacrifice) that prevented people traveling from afar—"all the nations" (both Jews and non-Jews)—from fully participating in worshiping God (see Is 56:7). The following day they head to the Temple again and discuss, through the symbol of a fig tree, the current reality of God's Chosen People, Israel.*

✳ Scripture Reading: Mark 11:1–25 ✳

Note: * In the Old Testament, Israel is often symbolized by a fig tree (see Jer 8:13, 24:1–8, 29:17; Hos 9:10; Jl 1:7).

Evening Prayer

Verse to Remember

> Jesus, Son of David, **have mercy on me!**
>
> —Mark 10:47

Respond to God's Word

 Find what Jesus does when he first enters the Temple.

 What might Jesus have seen or thought before leaving?

 Meditate: Jesus reminds Peter that God can restore his "withered" family, Israel. What big thing can you have faith in God to "unwither" in God's time?

Closing Prayer

Let us pray: Lord God, help us follow the example of your Son, who handed himself over to death out of love for us and the whole world. Through Jesus Christ, Our Lord. **Amen.**

Fourth Thursday of Lent

Morning Prayer

Psalm Verse

> Enter not into judgment with your servant; **for no man living is righteous before you.**
>
> —Psalm 143:2

Contemplate

The Son of God is both a judge and your advocate, meaning "lawyer" or "defender." Rest a moment secure in his faithful defense of you.

Jesus, Son of God, thank you for your never-ending, steadfast mercy that infinitely exceeds all of my failed attempts at my own righteousness.

Enter the Word of God

Introduction

On his third trip to the Temple, Jesus faces questions from the religious leaders regarding what authority he speaks and acts on. After they refuse to answer a question from Jesus, he tells them a parable whose negative implications they understand.

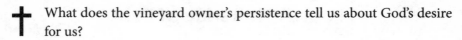 Scripture Reading: Mark 11:27–12:12 ✷

Evening Prayer

Verse to Remember

> Jesus, Son of David, **have mercy on me!**
>
> —Mark 10:47

Respond to God's Word

 What situation or discussion causes Jesus to tell the parable of the vineyard?

✝ What does the vineyard owner's persistence tell us about God's desire for us?

🕯 *Meditate:* God has an inheritance for you! It's not something we can earn, much less try to take by force. An inheritance can only be accepted as a gift. What can you more fully accept as a true inheritance from God?

Closing Prayer

Let us pray: Lord God, help us follow the example of your Son, who handed himself over to death out of love for us and the whole world. Through Jesus Christ, Our Lord. **Amen.**

Fourth Friday of Lent

Morning Prayer

Psalm Verse

> Behold, you desire truth in the inward being; **therefore teach me wisdom in my secret heart.**
>
> —Psalm 51:6

Contemplate

Open your innermost self so that God can give supernatural wisdom.

Lord our Teacher, give me the patience to seek and understand the wisdom of your kingdom.

Enter the Word of God

Introduction

In response to Jesus's parable, the Temple leaders send representatives of rival Jewish sects (Pharisees, Herodians, and Sadducees) to challenge him. In response, Jesus teaches them, offering a stinging critique of how these shepherds of Israel have strayed from God's will.

✷ Scripture Reading: Mark 12:13–34 ✷

Evening Prayer

Verse to Remember

> Jesus, Son of David, **have mercy on me!**
>
> —Mark 10:47

Respond to God's Word

 What three questions do people ask Jesus during this Temple scene? Which intrigues you the most? Why?

 What do Jesus's reactions to each of the three questions show you about him?

 Meditate: Ask Jesus a question in prayer, and listen for how the Holy Spirit might begin to guide you toward an answer.

Closing Prayer

Let us pray: Lord God, help us follow the example of your Son, who handed himself over to death out of love for us and the whole world. Through Jesus Christ, Our Lord. **Amen.**

Fourth Saturday of Lent

Morning Prayer

Psalm Verse

> For, behold, [O Lord], your enemies shall perish; **all evildoers shall be scattered.**
>
> —Psalm 92:9

Contemplate

God sees the evil in our world. He does not want evil, but in giving freedom to humanity, he permits it for a time. Yet God is also acting, disrupting evil in sometimes hidden and unexpected ways. Dwell in God's protection. Claim his special protection on behalf of those experiencing weakness, lowliness, or oppression.

God our Father, protect us from evil and let the true peace of your kingdom break through here on earth, more and more.

Enter the Word of God

Introduction

Jesus shifts from answering questions in the Temple to teaching, offering each message based on what his discourse with the religious leaders has shown. After teaching, he notes positively the actions of a poor widow who embodies his exhortation to give all of one's self to God.

✖ Scripture Reading: Mark 12:35–44 ✖

Evening Prayer

Verse to Remember

> Jesus, Son of David, **have mercy on me!**
>
> —Mark 10:47

Respond to God's Word

 What details strike you in this passage?

✝ What is Jesus showing about who the Messiah is or what the Messiah is like?

🕯 *Meditate:* Calling Jesus "Messiah" (Christ) can become so common that the meaning gets lost in our words. What does it mean to you that Jesus is your Messiah, your personal, long-awaited Christ?

Closing Prayer

Let us pray: Lord God, help us follow the example of your Son, who handed himself over to death out of love for us and the whole world. Through Jesus Christ, Our Lord. **Amen.**

Fifth Sunday of Lent

Morning Prayer

Psalm Verse

> Let Israel be glad in his Maker, **let the sons of Zion rejoice in their King!**
>
> —Psalm 149:2

Contemplate

Allow the deep joy of a personal relationship with God (not simply reflecting on what you know *about* God) to refresh your soul.

God our loving Maker and King, free me from distraction to find joy in you in every moment of my life.

Enter the Word of God

Introduction

Jesus departs from the Temple, never to return again (according to the post-Resurrection accounts). One of his disciples makes a seemingly offhand comment about the Temple, to which Jesus responds with a profound statement that provokes a question from Peter, James, John, and Andrew.

✳ Scripture Reading: Mark 13:1–4 ✳

Evening Prayer

Verse to Remember

> O Lord, be gracious to me; **heal me for I have sinned against you.**
>
> —Psalm 41:4

Respond to God's Word

 Find the remark of the unnamed disciple after Jesus leaves the Temple. What does this remark show about this disciple's mind and heart?

 How could Jesus's answer in verse 2 symbolically point to his death? Or the current state of God's Chosen People, Israel?

 Meditate: Approach Jesus privately with a question that is urgent or heavy on your heart.

Closing Prayer

Let us pray: Lord God, help us follow the example of your Son, who handed himself over to death out of love for us and the whole world. Through Jesus Christ, Our Lord. **Amen.**

Fifth Monday of Lent

Morning Prayer

Psalm Verse

> The God of glory thunders, the Lord, over the mighty waters. **The voice of the Lord is power; the voice of the Lord is splendor.**
>
> —Psalm 29:3b–4, NABRE

Contemplate

Consider God's glory, power, and splendor—in this world, and eternally.

Almighty God, your glory is unmistakable and yet mysterious. Grant me the grace to give you glory and see your glory unfolding.

Enter the Word of God

Introduction

Jesus answers Peter, James, John, and Andrew's question in one of his longest continuous sermons in all of Mark's gospel. In this final speech, Jesus tells the disciples of the signs that will mark the cosmic end times to come.* He also reassures them, telling them not to be alarmed or anxious; the Holy Spirit will be present and God's plan of salvation will continue to bear fruit.

✷ Scripture Reading: Mark 13:5–27 ✷

Evening Prayer

Verse to Remember

> O Lord, be gracious to me; **heal me for I have sinned against you.**
>
> —Psalm 41:4

Respond to God's Word

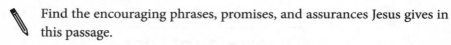

Find the encouraging phrases, promises, and assurances Jesus gives in this passage.

People who say "Look" are often a distraction from the reality that Jesus has revealed everything to us. What is that "everything" in a nutshell?

Meditate: Which encouragement or assurance from Jesus do you need to hear right now or in time of chaos or uncertainty? Allow Jesus's encouragement to sink into your heart.

Note: * Vivid descriptions of future events and/or the end times were not uncommon in first-century Judaism. This passage makes reference to Daniel 11:31, a prophecy of the destruction of the Temple. The Church understands that symbolic language and prophecies can be fulfilled multiple times. We are encouraged to avoid an unhealthy curiosity about predicting the future (see *CCC*, 2115), and to instead follow Jesus's assurances that his Second Coming will be so evident that no one will miss it. The Church teaches that before Christ's Second Coming and the fulfillment of God's plan through human history, the Church will pass through a final trial. Then the kingdom of God will be fulfilled through God's victory over this final unleashing of evil (see *CCC*, 675–677).

Closing Prayer

Let us pray: Almighty, ever-living God, who sent your son as our Savior to take flesh and submit to the Cross, fill our hearts with his grace. Through Jesus Christ, Our Lord. **Amen.**

Fifth Tuesday of Lent

Morning Prayer

Psalm Verse

> Our soul waits for the LORD; **he is our help and shield.**
>
> —Psalm 33:20

Contemplate

Imagine your soul waiting while God acts to help and shield you.

God, my shield, give me eyes to see the world and what you've entrusted to me with a new spirit of hope in times of waiting.

Enter the Word of God

Introduction

Jesus returns to the image of the fig tree for Israel, God's Chosen People, revealing God's patience with and providence for his people. Jesus exhorts his disciples to remain faithfully alert and watchful, to not tire of waiting for God's plan to be fulfilled.

✷ Scripture Reading: Mark 13:25–37 ✷

Evening Prayer

Verse to Remember

> O LORD, be gracious to me; **heal me for I have sinned against you.**
>
> —Psalm 41:4

Respond to God's Word

 What is Jesus pointing out about the relationship between a tree's fruit and the seasons of the year?

 What kind of trust would a homeowner need to have in his servants to go away for a long time and give them the authority and resources to carry out their tasks? See verse 34.

 Meditate: How does it feel to be so trusted by God that he would leave you in charge of particular things as his steward while you wait for his return?

Closing Prayer

Let us pray: Almighty, ever-living God, who sent your son as our Savior to take flesh and submit to the Cross, fill our hearts with his grace. Through Jesus Christ, Our Lord. **Amen.**

Fifth Wednesday of Lent

Morning Prayer

Psalm Verse

[The children of men] feast on the abundance of your house,
and you give them drink from the river of your delights.
—Psalm 36:8

Contemplate

Imagine drinking in, soaking in, being washed in the rushing, flowing river of God's delight.

Jesus, free my heart to respond to who you are from the depths of the unique, beautiful soul you have formed in me.

Enter the Word of God

Introduction

As the pilgrimage festival of Passover, which brings Jews from all over to Jerusalem, approaches, some religious leaders, and even one of Jesus's Twelve, are plotting against Jesus. In contrast, another humble woman shows a true disciple's response to Jesus's presence.

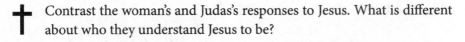 Scripture Reading: Mark 14:1–11 ✳

Evening Prayer

Verse to Remember

> O Lord, be gracious to me; **heal me for I have sinned against you.**
>
> —Psalm 41:4

Respond to God's Word

 How do you think the people at dinner might have felt about the woman?

✝ Contrast the woman's and Judas's responses to Jesus. What is different about who they understand Jesus to be?

Meditate: Both the woman in the treasury scene at the Temple (see Mk 12:41–44) and this woman in Bethany are fully surrendering their lives without looking back. Is there something in your life you can give "all the way" to Jesus?

Closing Prayer

Let us pray: Almighty, ever-living God, who sent your son as our Savior to take flesh and submit to the Cross, fill our hearts with his grace. Through Jesus Christ, Our Lord. **Amen.**

Fifth Thursday of Lent

Morning Prayer

Psalm Verse

> In the shadow of your wings I will take refuge, **till the storms of destruction pass by.**
>
> —Psalm 57:1b

Contemplate

Think about Jesus, who not only gives refuge but also makes himself truly our brother, taking refuge in God the Father when his soul experiences sorrow.

God, whatever the storm, let me huddle under your protective wing as you allow storms to exist yet pass me by.

Enter the Word of God

Introduction

The Passover festival has finally begun! Jesus shares the Passover fellowship meal with the Twelve, an opportunity for repentance that future betrayer Judas chooses not to accept.

✳ Scripture Reading: Mark 14:12–26 ✳

Evening Prayer

Verse to Remember

> O Lord, be gracious to me; **heal me for I have sinned against you.**
>
> —Psalm 41:4

Respond to God's Word

 Find an example of Jesus showing his friendship with his future betrayer.

 No sin is too large or awful for Jesus's mercy and forgiveness. How does Jesus still offer space for repentance, a change of heart from his betrayer?

 Meditate: In the Old Testament, covenants were sealed by animal blood. Jesus offers his blood for a new family relationship that extends God's Chosen People beyond Israel to all, including you. Pause to dwell and rest in your place as part of God's family, in a covenant sealed and ratified by blood.

Closing Prayer

Let us pray: Almighty, ever-living God, who sent your son as our Savior to take flesh and submit to the Cross, fill our hearts with his grace. Through Jesus Christ, Our Lord. **Amen.**

Fifth Friday of Lent

Morning Prayer

Psalm Verse

The sacrifice acceptable to God is a broken spirit; **a broken and contrite heart, O God, you will not despise.**

—Psalm 51:17

Contemplate

God is not interested in mere gestures or material offerings. God sees and loves your heart, your truest self, even in times of failure.

Lord God, give me the strength to know that your forgiveness and mercy are greater than even the deepest sin.

Enter the Word of God

Introduction

Later that night, after the Passover meal in the garden of Gethsemane, Jesus's other disciples begin to follow Judas in lesser ways, starting to drift away* from closely following Jesus. Jesus echoes his teaching of chapter 13 to remain faithfully alert and watchful.

✠ Scripture Reading: Mark 14:27–46 ✠

Evening Prayer

Verse to Remember

> O Lord, be gracious to me; **heal me for I have sinned against you.**
>
> —Psalm 41:4

Respond to God's Word

Find an example of how Jesus's guidance to watch and not fall asleep during a time of chaos (see Mk 13) is repeated here.

Judas calls Jesus a word translated as "Rabbi" or "Master." What does his using terms of earthly authority, and not "Lord" or "Messiah," show about how he misunderstands Jesus?

Meditate: Jesus is deeply troubled in his heart, but acts boldly, going directly into the hands of his betrayer. Allow Jesus's love and desire to save give you the confident assurance that Jesus will not lose you or leave you.

Closing Prayer

Let us pray: Almighty, ever-living God, who sent your son as our Savior to take flesh and submit to the Cross, fill our hearts with his grace. Through Jesus Christ, Our Lord. **Amen.**

Note: * In Greek, the word repeated in verses 27 and 29 is *skandalizomai* (like the English word *scandalize*), meaning to stumble or fall away.

Fifth Saturday of Lent

Morning Prayer

Psalm Verse

> Great is his mercy toward us; **and the faithfulness of the
> LORD endures for ever. Praise the Lord!**
>
> —Psalm 117:2

Contemplate

Dwell upon Jesus's faithfulness to you and his Father.

*Jesus, you are our Christ, our Messiah, our rescuer, because of your faithfulness
to God's plan of salvation, despite all of the suffering you endured. Thank you.*

Enter the Word of God

Introduction

After Jesus's arrest late at night in Gethsemane, all of his disciples rapidly
disperse. Jesus is then taken to an unusual middle-of-the-night meeting at the
high priest's home, where other religious leaders and a portion of the Sanhedrin* have gathered to plot what to do next.

✳ Scripture Reading: Mark 14:46–65 ✳

Evening Prayer

Verse to Remember

> O LORD, be gracious to me; **heal me for I have sinned against
> you.**
>
> —Psalm 41:4

Note: * The Sanhedrin was a religious council of Jews to whom the Romans
gave some status and authority to rule the Jewish minority in Jerusalem and
the surrounding areas. The Sanhedrin typically met at the Temple.

Respond to God's Word

 What stands out to you in today's passage?

✝ Why do you think the chief priests and the Sanhedrin do not believe that Jesus is really the Messiah? Are the reasons people do not believe Jesus is the Messiah similar or different today?

Meditate: What do you look forward to about the future spoken of in verse 62? Praise and adore God for this.

Closing Prayer

Let us pray: Almighty, ever-living God, who sent your son as our Savior to take flesh and submit to the Cross, fill our hearts with his grace. Through Jesus Christ, Our Lord. **Amen.**

Palm Sunday

Morning Prayer

Psalm Verse

> Out of my distress I called on the LORD; **the LORD answered me and set me free.**
>
> —Psalm 118:5

Contemplate

God sees you even in times of distress, anguish, or anxiety.

God our Father, be not only my rescuer but also a healer—the one who restores all situations to rightness.

Enter the Word of God

Introduction

As the overnight discussions continue inside the high priest's house, Peter, still nearby, is confronted. Asked if he is one of Jesus's followers, Peter demonstrates through his words that he has abandoned Jesus, and breaks down afterward.

✴ Scripture Reading: Mark 14:66–72 ✴

Evening Prayer

Verse to Remember

> He bore the punishment that makes us whole, **by his wounds we were healed.**
>
> —Isaiah 53:5b, NABRE

Respond to God's Word

 What emotions might Peter have experienced during the questioning?

✝ Jesus knows our sins and allows us to freely choose every decision in our life. What does it show us about God that Jesus forgives Peter, one of his closest followers, and makes Peter the leader of the early church?

Meditate: Dwell in the reality that your deepest sin was not only forgiven when you asked but also forgotten and wiped away by God.

Closing Prayer

Let us pray: Almighty, ever-living God, who sent your son as our Savior to take flesh and submit to the Cross, fill our hearts with his grace. Through Jesus Christ, Our Lord. **Amen.**

Monday of Holy Week

Morning Prayer

Psalm Verse

> I say to God, my rock: "Why have you forgotten me? **Why do**
> **I go mourning because of the oppression of the enemy?"**
> —Psalm 42:9

Contemplate

Imagine all the emotions Jesus felt—his patience, restraint, sadness, frustration, and more—as he endured the insults and the process leading up to his death.

Lord Jesus, Son of God and Son of man, give me the courage to trust in God even when circumstances around me are out of my control.

Enter the Word of God

Introduction

The religious leaders who orchestrated the meeting at the high priest's home then convene the entire Sanhedrin in the early morning hours to deliver* Jesus to the Roman governor, Pilate. He has the legal authority to issue a death sentence for treason against the secular government, a power the Jewish religious leaders lack. Pilate keeps peace between the Jewish minority and the Roman government he represents by satisfying the desires of the crowd during their religious feast.

✶ Scripture Reading: Mark 15:1–15 ✶

Evening Prayer

Verse to Remember

> He bore the punishment that makes us whole, **by his wounds**
> **we were healed.**
> —Isaiah 53:5b, NABRE

Note: * *Deliver* literally means "hand over," the same word as *betray* in Greek, which is used in verse 15.

Respond to God's Word

 What seems suspicious or unusual about the Sanhedrin's actions over the past night? How do you think a governing council would more normally behave?

 Do you think the chief priests are envious of Jesus just because of his popularity, or is there something more?

 Meditate: The back and forth in this scene centers on "the King of the Jews," a political title. Jesus's name means "the Lord saves." Pray about what this means for you personally.

Closing Prayer

Let us pray: O God, grant that we may draw, from the mystery of Christ's sacrifice for all eternity, the fullness of love and life. Through Jesus Christ, Our Lord. **Amen.**

Tuesday of Holy Week

Morning Prayer

Psalm Verse

Why do I go mourning because of the oppression of the enemy? **Oh, send out your light and your truth; let them lead me.**

—Psalm 43:2b–3a

Contemplate

Jesus knows, understands, and enters the true horror and agony of death (see *CCC*, 612). Though he may seem far away when we are experiencing mourning, sorrow, and shock over a personal tragedy, Jesus is as close to us as ever.

Jesus, my brother and friend, send your light and truth into my places of greatest darkness. Give me the hope that you held to in your worst moments of trial.

Enter the Word of God

Introduction

The purposefully long and slow process of execution* by crucifixion begins. In the Roman Empire, this form of punishment was reserved for those convicted of treason or the most serious crimes. Executions were deliberately public and highly visible events in order to maintain control of the population.

�֎ Scripture Reading: Mark 15:16–32 ✖

Evening Prayer

Verse to Remember

> He bore the punishment that makes us whole, **by his wounds we were healed.**
>
> —Isaiah 53:5b, NABRE

Respond to God's Word

 Both Gentiles and Jews mock and insult Jesus during his brutal execution. What might it have been like for Simon of Cyrene to carry Jesus's Cross in this heated situation?

✝ Why doesn't Jesus rescue himself, as those taunting him suggest?

 Meditate: The Jewish religious leaders claimed they would believe that Jesus was the Christ if Jesus did rescue himself. What does it do to us when we put conditions or limitations on who Jesus is or what Jesus can do? Ask the Lord to show you how to let go of the limits you might place on him.

Closing Prayer

Let us pray: O God, grant that we may draw, from the mystery of Christ's sacrifice for all eternity, the fullness of love and life. Through Jesus Christ, Our Lord. **Amen.**

Note: * The English word *excruciating* comes from the same root word as *crucifixion*.

Wednesday of Holy Week

Morning Prayer

Psalm Verse

Your way, O God, is holy. **What god is great like our God?**
—Psalm 77:13

Contemplate

Consider the shocking, scandalous uniqueness of the Son of God, who allows himself to be killed, to be executed, for our sake.

Jesus, Son of God, you are great beyond human understanding. Your choice to give yourself over to death, without the protection of earthly or divine powers you could have called upon, is an act of pure love.

Enter the Word of God

Introduction

Crucifixions typically ended with the prisoner dying by suffocation. In his final breaths, Jesus prays part of Psalm 22 and then dies—a fulfillment of Mark 13:24–26. A leader of Roman soldiers (a Gentile) is the first person in Mark's gospel to declare Jesus the "Son of God"—the key message Mark had given us, his audience, in his very first verse.

✠ Scripture Reading: Mark 15:33–39 ✠

Evening Prayer

Verse to Remember

He bore the punishment that makes us whole, **by his wounds we were healed.**
—Isaiah 53:5b, NABRE

Respond to God's Word

 What do you think the centurion sees or experiences that makes him, an experienced soldier who has overseen many crucifixions and is not even Jewish, declare that Jesus really is the Son of God?

✝ Are you surprised that this first, very clear and open proclamation after Jesus's death comes from a Gentile? Why or why not? What does this reveal about God's plan for his people?

Meditate: What does it mean to you that God went to these lengths to restore and rescue humanity from sin for all time?

Closing Prayer

Let us pray: O God, grant that we may draw, from the mystery of Christ's sacrifice for all eternity, the fullness of love and life. Through Jesus Christ, Our Lord. **Amen.**

Thursday of Holy Week

Morning Prayer

Psalm Verse

Restore us, O God; **let your face shine, that we may be saved!**
—Psalm 80:3

Contemplate

Allow the shining brightness of God's face, revealed in Jesus, to warm you like the radiant sun.

O God, my daily life includes so many ups and downs, so many different emotions, so many uncertainties—renew and restore my heart and mind. Bring me relief and peace.

Enter the Word of God

Introduction

At this moment of Jesus's death, every single one of his male disciples has fallen away, yet many women are still watching.

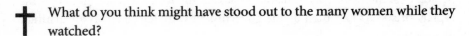

✷ Scripture Reading: Mark 15:40–41 ✷

Evening Prayer

Verse to Remember

> He bore the punishment that makes us whole, **by his wounds we were healed.**
>
> —Isaiah 53:5b, NABRE

Respond to God's Word

 Find the verbs that describe Salome's connection to Jesus.

✝ What do you think might have stood out to the many women while they watched?

🕯 *Meditate:* The women have chosen to follow Jesus as he truly is—a Messiah who saves through his own sacrifice. When did you first see Jesus for who he truly is and make a decision to be his disciple?

Closing Prayer

Let us pray: O God, grant that we may draw, from the mystery of Christ's sacrifice for all eternity, the fullness of love and life. Through Jesus Christ, Our Lord. **Amen.**

Good Friday

Morning Prayer

Psalm Verse

> Deliver me from death, O God, O God of my salvation, **and my tongue will sing aloud of your deliverance.**
>
> —Psalm 51:14

Contemplate

Imagine God as the rescuer, the one who delivers you from guilt and death.

Christ Jesus, you truly experienced and entered into death itself out of love for me. Help me embrace you, and you alone, as my salvation.

Enter the Word of God

Introduction

Joseph is a member of the Sanhedrin* from the village of Arimathea. He is a person of some wealth, as he has access to a tomb for Jesus's burial. In contrast, typical prisoners executed by the government were left to rot as a warning to others.

✳ Scripture Reading: Mark 15:42–47 ✳

Evening Prayer

Verse to Remember

> He bore the punishment that makes us whole, **by his wounds we were healed.**
>
> —Isaiah 53:5b, NABRE

Note: * The Church teaches that the circumstances of Jesus's trial and execution are historically complex and that "the personal sin of the participants (Judas, the Sanhedrin, Pilate) is known to God alone" (CCC, 597). It is wrong to place collective responsibility on the Jewish people or any subgroup of Jews, such as the Sanhedrin, Pharisees, and scribes. See also CCC, 574–576, 839–840.

Respond to God's Word

 What trait of Joseph of Arimathea stands out to you in how he models being a disciple of Jesus?

✝ What symbolic meaning do you find in the timing of Jesus being raised from the dead during the Sabbath—the day when God rested over his creation?

Meditate: Joseph was a member of the Sanhedrin yet was drawn to follow Jesus with concrete actions. Have you ever experienced a draw to do something that would lead to questions from peers? Prayerfully reflect on that experience.

Closing Prayer

Let us pray: Remember your mercies, O God, and with your eternal protection sanctify me, your servant. Through Jesus Christ, Our Lord. **Amen.**

Saturday of Holy Week

Morning Prayer

Psalm Verse

> Then all men will fear; **they will tell what God has wrought,**
> **and ponder what he has done.**
> —Psalm 64:9

Contemplate

Biblical fear of the Lord is different from simply being scared or afraid; it is a reverent awe of the stunning power of God, like the gasp of awe one might experience when seeing a massive waterfall or a great cliff up close. Contemplate Jesus's death and Resurrection with this sense of fear and pondering.

O God, your work inspires awe in my deepest soul; allow this to flow out into my life so that I can share my relationship with you with others more freely.

Enter the Word of God

Introduction

Early on Sunday morning, some of Jesus's disciples who had witnessed his death go to anoint Jesus's body in his burial tomb.* Upon hearing that Jesus has risen from the dead, the women are (literally in Greek in verse 8) ecstatic! After sharing a meal of fellowship, showing forgiveness and reconciliation, the Eleven are sent on a mission to continue to act in Jesus's name, drawing all people to God.

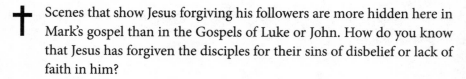

✠ Scripture Reading: Mark 16:1–20 ✠

Evening Prayer

Verse to Remember

> He bore the punishment that makes us whole, **by his wounds we were healed.**
>
> —Isaiah 53:5b, NABRE

Respond to God's Word

Find words that describe the women's reactions to Jesus's Resurrection.

Scenes that show Jesus forgiving his followers are more hidden here in Mark's gospel than in the Gospels of Luke or John. How do you know that Jesus has forgiven the disciples for their sins of disbelief or lack of faith in him?

Meditate: To believe in God's love is the most important, foundational, fundamental decision of a person's life (see Pope Benedict XVI, *Deus Caritas Est*). Jesus is a true friend. He does not force himself upon us; he simply invites us, again and again, to welcome him into the center of our lives, putting aside our own self-reliance and trusting in the power and grace of the Holy Spirit.

Note: * His anointing by a woman in Mark 14:3–8 prefigured this event.

Have you said yes to Jesus's invitation? Have you asked him to fill your heart and bring you into his kingdom, now and for eternity? If you are not sure, why not make that fundamental decision today? Ask Jesus to renew his Spirit in your life, to strengthen and cleanse your heart through the sacraments, and to remain with you forever so that you can be his follower and live out his will for your life.

Closing Prayer

Let us pray: God, inflame us with heavenly desires, that with minds made pure we may attain festivities of unending splendor. Through Jesus Christ, Our Lord. **Amen.**

Easter: Acts of the Apostles

Starting Simply

Acts of the Apostles reveals how Jesus's early followers lived "the Way" of Jesus in the thirty years following his Ascension. Acts was written as a sequel to his gospel by Luke, a gentile believer who wrote in eloquent, highly educated Greek and was a companion to Paul.* The word *acts* is a translation of the Greek word *praxeis*. A *praxis* was a genre of historical biography to show people how to follow the example of a notable person's practices.

Jesus is fully God *and* fully human, and so to put Jesus's example into practice, his followers must rely on the guidance and power that comes from the indwelling presence of the Holy Spirit. To those first Christians, the Holy Spirit brought "the full commissioning and equipping needed to spread the Good News of salvation," and in just a few decades, as Lavinia Spirito observes in her commentary in the *Living the Word Catholic Women's Bible*, this "minor Jewish sect composed largely of uneducated, Aramaic-speaking Palestinian Jews" spread God's plan of salvation to the ends of the known world, "turning the world upside down" in the process.[1] Luke's inspired words reveal that we can depend upon God to send the Spirit in abundance to lead us as followers of Jesus in *any* era.

Note: * See Acts 1:1–3 for reference to a first book and Luke 1:1–4 to compare the introductions for the similarities that lead to a scholarly consensus that these books were written by the same human author.

Easter Sunday

Morning Prayer

Psalm Verse

> Let the faithful exult in glory; **let them sing for joy on their couches.**
>
> —Psalm 149:5

Contemplate

God invites you to rejoice in his glory from a place of restful, relaxing comfort as his beloved child, a place the psalmist describes as comfy as a "couch." Dwell safe and secure in God's comfort.

Lord, allow me to find new, true rejoicing in your saving death and Resurrection.

Enter the Word of God

Introduction

Luke the evangelist picks up right where he left off at the end of his gospel, with the eleven apostles waiting for Jesus to initiate God's kingdom in a new way. Jesus gives a bold projection of how the Holy Spirit will work through his followers, a geographic spread that unfolds over the next three decades in this book.

✷ Scripture Reading: Acts 1:1–11 ✷

Evening Prayer

Verse to Remember

> This is the day which the LORD has made; **let us rejoice and be glad in it, alleluia.**
>
> —Psalm 118:24

Respond to God's Word

 Jesus's followers see his resurrected body and hear his teaching for forty days after God raises Jesus from the dead. Find the question they ask Jesus.

 Why do you think they ask this question at this moment?

 Meditate: How would you have felt in the first century hearing verse 8? Ask the Lord in prayer in what places he has plans for you to be a witness for him.

Closing Prayer

Let us pray: O God, on this day you have conquered death and unlocked for us the path to eternity. Give us the renewal brought by your Spirit. We ask this through Jesus Christ, Our Lord. **Amen.**

First Monday of Easter

Morning Prayer

Psalm Verse

> Sing to the LORD a new song, **his praise in the assembly of the faithful!**
>
> —Psalm 149:1b

Contemplate

You are not alone. You belong to an assembly, a gathering God has called together of those who place their hope in him. Soak in the encouragement of all holy men and women praying with you right now, in Christ Jesus, our head.

Jesus, you are the Head of your Body, the Church. Help me place my trust in you as you lead us to your eternal perfection.

Enter the Word of God

Introduction

After Jesus ascends, the apostles take an important step in continuing what Jesus began in them* by selecting a replacement for the "office" vacated by Judas (verse 20). The Greek for "office," *episkope*, with *epi* meaning "over" and *skope* meaning "see," is the source of the English terms *bishop* and *episcopacy*. Following Jesus's example not to condemn one another and acknowledging that we cannot know another person's heart, the Church does not teach that Judas is eternally separated from God ("in hell").

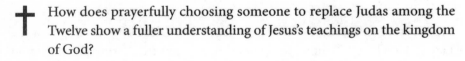

✳ Scripture Reading: Acts 1:12–26 ✳

Evening Prayer

Verse to Remember

> This is the day which the LORD has made; **let us rejoice and be glad in it, alleluia.**
>
> —Psalm 118:24

Respond to God's Word

 Find the written source Peter turns to for insight into understanding Judas's actions and what to do next.

✝ How does prayerfully choosing someone to replace Judas among the Twelve show a fuller understanding of Jesus's teachings on the kingdom of God?

🕯 *Meditate:* Think of a decision you face right now, large or small; pray to God for guidance, and hand the burden over to him.

Note: * See Jesus's promises about the Twelve in Matthew 19:28 and Luke 22:30. In the ancient world, "judging" referred to general governance (like the Old Testament's Book of Judges, meaning "rulers"), not the specific judicial role of making decisions in a court.

Closing Prayer

Let us pray: God of mercy, kindle our faith so that we may understand more deeply in what font we have been washed, by whose Spirit we have been reborn, and by whose Blood we have been redeemed. Through Jesus Christ, Our Lord. **Amen.**

First Tuesday of Easter

Morning Prayer

Psalm Verse

> For the LORD takes pleasure in his people; **he adorns the humble with victory.**
>
> —Psalm 149:4

Contemplate

Receive the gaze of your Lord, who delights in you and all those united to Christ.

Lord, open my heart to the signs, wonders, and joys you want me to see.

Enter the Word of God

Introduction

Like Passover, Pentecost was a pilgrimage feast, celebrating God's gift of the Law to Israel on Mt. Sinai, for which Jewish men from around the Roman Empire would come to Jerusalem. On Pentecost, just ten days after the Ascension, the signs of God's profound revelation to his people are present just as they were on Mt. Sinai; Peter takes the lead to articulate how God's promises in the Hebrew Scriptures are being fulfilled.

✠ Scripture Reading: Acts 2:1–24 ✠

Evening Prayer

Verse to Remember

> This is the day which the Lord has made; **let us rejoice and be glad in it, alleluia.**
>
> —Psalm 118:24

Respond to God's Word

 Find the written source Peter turns to for insight to understand this strange occurrence on the annual Jewish pilgrimage feast of Pentecost.

 What does God reveal to be new and different about this period of "last days" (verse 17) from Jesus's Ascension to when he returns?

 Meditate: Jesus was not defeated by death but won victory over death itself. Do you believe that Jesus will raise you from the dead if you remain in him? How does it make you feel? Meditate on verse 24 in prayer. Share your joys and hesitations with the Lord.

Closing Prayer

Let us pray: God of mercy, kindle our faith so that we may understand more deeply in what font we have been washed, by whose Spirit we have been reborn, and by whose Blood we have been redeemed. Through Jesus Christ, Our Lord. **Amen.**

First Wednesday of Easter

Morning Prayer

Psalm Verse

> Let Israel be glad in his Maker, **let the sons of Zion rejoice in their King!**
>
> —Psalm 149:2

Contemplate

Ponder how deeply a "Maker" knows his creation. Allow God to know you intimately in this moment.

Lord God, you are our Maker, and you still desire to sustain us through your Holy Spirit. Send me your peace.

Enter the Word of God

Introduction

Peter continues his teaching, interpreting the scriptures* to the thousands of Jews present. His message ends with a clear call to action: every person has the free choice to say yes to baptism for the forgiveness of sins and enter into a new life as a disciple of Jesus, the Risen Savior, where individuals are united in Christ's Body—visible through the "breaking of the bread" (the Eucharist), the teaching of the Church through the apostles and their successors, and the prayers of the Church.

✳ Scripture Reading: Acts 2:24–47 ✳

Evening Prayer

Verse to Remember

> This is the day which the LORD has made; **let us rejoice and be glad in it, alleluia.**
>
> —Psalm 118:24

Note: * This refers only to the books of the Old Testament, as the New Testament was not yet written when Peter preached.

Respond to God's Word

 What does verse 33 reveal to you about what Jesus is doing now that he has been taken up to God's right hand?

 Who should be baptized and why?

Meditate: Reflect on verses 42–43. Have the teachings of the apostles transmitted by the Holy Spirit, life in faith shared with others, or the Eucharist (the "breaking of the bread") brought you awe, comfort, or encouragement? If necessary, ask God for healing in any of these areas of being part of his family.

Closing Prayer

Let us pray: God of mercy, kindle our faith so that we may understand more deeply in what font we have been washed, by whose Spirit we have been reborn, and by whose Blood we have been redeemed. Through Jesus Christ, Our Lord. **Amen.**

First Thursday of Easter

Morning Prayer

Psalm Verse

> For you have been my help, **and in the shadow of your wings**
> **I sing for joy.**
> —Psalm 63:7

Contemplate

Visualize God, your divine help, giving you shade and protection underneath wings as strong and majestic as a large bird's.

God, every time I might think I am doing something myself, you are always there helping me, lifting me up. Thank you for allowing me to cooperate in your work.

Enter the Word of God

Introduction

At this point the vast majority of Jesus's disciples are Jewish, so after the Resurrection they continue to worship at the Temple and participate in Temple life. A man with a disability,* who must beg to survive due to being excluded from society and work, asks Peter and John for alms, which leads to healing through faith in Jesus.

✳ Scripture Reading: Acts 3:1–12 ✳

Evening Prayer

Verse to Remember

> This is the day which the LORD has made; **let us rejoice and be glad in it, alleluia.**
>
> —Psalm 118:24

Respond to God's Word

 What stands out to you in this passage?

What do Peter and John say and do to the man who cannot walk?

Meditate: What characteristics do Peter, John, and the man who is healed demonstrate that you would like to emulate? Ask God for the gifts and attitudes that you long for.

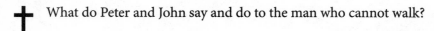

Note: * In ancient Near Eastern cultures, people with disabilities were considered inferior and lacking full human dignity; they were identified by their disability ("lame" or "crippled"). Today, the Church teaches that disability is neither shameful nor a stigma, and that social "structures of sin," such as unjust discrimination against or exclusion of people with disabilities, must be "transformed into structures of solidarity" (*Compendium of the Social Doctrine of the Church*, 193).

Closing Prayer

Let us pray: God of mercy, kindle our faith so that we may understand more deeply in what font we have been washed, by whose Spirit we have been reborn, and by whose Blood we have been redeemed. Through Jesus Christ, Our Lord. **Amen.**

First Friday of Easter

Morning Prayer

Psalm Verse

> My soul is feasted as with marrow and fat, **and my mouth praises you with joyful lips.**
>
> —Psalm 63:5

Contemplate

Imagine the Lord nourishing you with the exact right types of food for your soul today.

Jesus, help me never be overwhelmed by the richness of the faith you infuse through the Holy Spirit but to find in those riches what I need for my life.

Enter the Word of God

Introduction

Many other Jews worshiping at the Temple witnessed this miraculous healing in the name of Jesus the Christ. Peter seizes this opportunity to tell them about God's plan of salvation, culminating in Jesus the Messiah, sent by God to invite all to repent and be reconciled to God through the forgiveness of sins.

✠ Scripture Reading: Acts 3:11–26 ✠

Evening Prayer

Verse to Remember

> This is the day which the Lord has made; **let us rejoice and be glad in it, alleluia.**
>
> —Psalm 118:24

Respond to God's Word

 Peter gives many reasons why the crowd of fellow Israelites should not be so shocked. Find a reason that is compelling to you.

✝ Why does Peter bring up events and people from Israel's history in his explanation?

Meditate: Verse 19 invites you to refreshment from experiencing the presence of the Lord. Ask God to give you this refreshment and comfort of his presence where you most need it.

Closing Prayer

Let us pray: God of mercy, kindle our faith so that we may understand more deeply in what font we have been washed, by whose Spirit we have been reborn, and by whose Blood we have been redeemed. Through Jesus Christ, Our Lord. **Amen.**

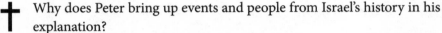

First Saturday of Easter

Morning Prayer

Psalm Verse

> So I will bless you as long as I live; **I will lift up my hands and call on your name.**
>
> —Psalm 63:4

Contemplate

As you bless God with your life, God's Holy Spirit is filling you with more of his grace, to overflow to others.

Lord, take my words, work, and worries—my entire life—as a blessing. Fill my heart with your Holy Spirit to praise your name in all that I do.

Enter the Word of God

Introduction

Not everyone is pleased with Peter's impromptu teaching on how God's plan has been revealed through Israel's history. Some of the Jewish leaders become upset and arrest Peter and John. Filled with the Holy Spirit, Peter continues to proclaim to them the Good News that Jesus is the one and only savior of the world.

✷ Scripture Reading: Acts 4:1–12 ✷

Evening Prayer

Verse to Remember

> This is the day which the Lord has made; **let us rejoice and be glad in it, alleluia.**
>
> —Psalm 118:24

Respond to God's Word

 Find precisely who gets upset that Peter and John are teaching their fellow Jews. What do you think upsets them?

 Jesus means "God saves." What does Jesus do for us?

 Meditate: Reflect on Jesus as the cornerstone. How does he play this role in your life?

Closing Prayer

Let us pray: God of mercy, kindle our faith so that we may understand more deeply in what font we have been washed, by whose Spirit we have been reborn, and by whose Blood we have been redeemed. Through Jesus Christ, Our Lord. **Amen.**

Second Sunday of Easter

Morning Prayer

Psalm Verse

> My soul clings to you; **your right hand upholds me.**
>
> —Psalm 63:8

Contemplate

God seeks you and holds you tight, no matter what the situation.

Holy Spirit, pour into me the strength, gifts, and words for handling difficult situations.

Enter the Word of God

Introduction

The Sanhedrin and religious scholars are amazed by the knowledge of the scriptures and God demonstrated by Peter and John, seemingly ordinary men. They are conflicted over how to react, concerned that publicly punishing Peter and John would displease all who witnessed or heard about the miracle.

✠ Scripture Reading: Acts 4:8–22 ✠

Evening Prayer

Verse to Remember

> Jesus was carried up into heaven. **And the disciples worshiped him, and returned to Jerusalem with great joy.**
>
> —cf. Luke 24:51–52

Respond to God's Word

 Find the Jewish leaders' main concern and aim once Peter, filled with the Holy Spirit, has spoken and explained himself.

By becoming human, Jesus made it possible for us to share in his divine life. How do we see this in Peter's life?

Meditate: Have you experienced a desire to speak of or share an encounter with God that you've had? Recount that experience, and tell the Lord what you most cherish from it, or ask him to make himself known to you in a personal way in the coming week.

Closing Prayer

Let us pray: God of mercy, kindle our faith so that we may understand more deeply in what font we have been washed, by whose Spirit we have been reborn, and by whose Blood we have been redeemed. Through Jesus Christ, Our Lord. **Amen.**

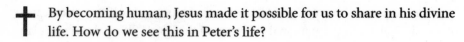

Second Monday of Easter

Morning Prayer

Psalm Verse

> Hope in God; for I shall again praise him, **my help and my God.**
>
> —Psalm 42:11b

Contemplate

Think about God preparing to give you a new outpouring of praise-filled prayer.

Lord God, be my divine helper. Give me a secure hope in your ultimate plan for my life.

Enter the Word of God

Introduction

The community of believers responds to Peter and John's return by joining together to pray. Praying together, the community experiences more signs of the Holy Spirit and the personal presence of the Spirit filling them more and more, resulting in boldness to proclaim God's plan.

Scripture Reading: Acts 4:23–31

Evening Prayer

Verse to Remember

> Jesus was carried up into heaven. **And the disciples worshiped him, and returned to Jerusalem with great joy.**
>
> —cf. Luke 24:51–52

Respond to God's Word

What words of the community's prayer stand out to you?

How is the Holy Spirit the "giver of life" to the many people we hear of being filled with the Holy Spirit?

Meditate: Ask the Lord to fill your heart with the Holy Spirit, for boldness in an area of your life.

Closing Prayer

Let us pray: O God, let us exult forever in renewed youthfulness of spirit that we may look forward in confident hope to the rejoicing of the day of Resurrection. Through Jesus Christ, Our Lord. **Amen.**

Second Tuesday of Easter

Morning Prayer

Psalm Verse

> To you all flesh will come with its burden of sin. **Too heavy for us, our offenses, but you wipe them away.**
> —Psalm 65:2b–3, Liturgy of the Hours translation

Contemplate

Offer all of your burdens and uncertainties to God. No sin that we present to God is too large or insignificant for God's forgiveness.

God our Father, you run to us, your children, to embrace us and lift our burdens. Give me the courage to not hold back or hide anything from you.

Enter the Word of God

Introduction

Luke highlights the positive example of Joseph (renamed Barnabas), who voluntarily sells his property and donates the proceeds to the community of believers.* Barnabas is directly contrasted with a married couple, Ananias and Sapphira, who desire to appear generous, thinking that this external appearance alone will please God or impress others, and who lie to achieve this. God forgives the sins of all who call on him. But God gives us free will, and when we choose not to accept God's love, we remain captive to the Evil One, who brings death.

✷ Scripture Reading: Acts 4:32–5:16 ✷

Note: * 5:11 is Luke's first use of the word *church*, which in Greek (*ekklesia*) was used to describe those whom God called out and gathered into the assembly of his people.

Evening Prayer

Verse to Remember

> Jesus was carried up into heaven. **And the disciples wor-**
> **shiped him, and returned to Jerusalem with great joy.**
> —cf. Luke 24:51–52

Respond to God's Word

 Find what aspect of Jesus's life the apostles share when they give their testimony (also known as "witness").

 How is verse 32a an image of God's plan for his family, united in the Lord?

 Meditate: Grace is God's own divine nature working in us. Luke notes that grace was upon the apostles as they testified. Turn to God to reflect on when you have experienced his grace in a noticeable way, or ask the Holy Spirit to pour out God's grace for what you need right now.

Closing Prayer

Let us pray: O God, let us exult forever in renewed youthfulness of spirit that we may look forward in confident hope to the rejoicing of the day of Resurrection. Through Jesus Christ, Our Lord. **Amen.**

Second Wednesday of Easter

Morning Prayer

Psalm Verse

> [The Lord] preserves the lives of his saints; **he delivers them**
> **from the hand of the wicked.**
> —Psalm 97:10b

Contemplate

A saint is someone who is set apart by God, whom God is making holy. Everyone in the Body of Christ is this type of saint (in contrast to a canonized saint, specifically identified by the Church for miraculous intercession). Contemplate the Lord preserving you, ripening you, sustaining you, and making you holy.

Lord, real obstacles from others and obstacles I create for myself can prevent me from doing your will. Reassure me constantly that you have a plan for me and are making a path, delivering me from obstacles as I follow you.

Enter the Word of God

Introduction

The apostles continue talking about Jesus the Messiah despite the warnings of the Sanhedrin. As a result, the Jewish leaders become more concerned and more jealous, and decide to arrest the apostles for teaching in the Temple.

✠ Scripture Reading: Acts 5:17–26 ✠

Evening Prayer

Verse to Remember

> Jesus was carried up into heaven. **And the disciples worshipped him, and returned to Jerusalem with great joy.**
>
> —cf. Luke 24:51–52

Respond to God's Word

Imagine you are worshiping in the Temple when the apostles enter. What would you find appealing about their teaching?

The Sadducees (who did not believe there would be any resurrection of the dead) are really indignant about the growth in the number of Jesus's followers. Why is professing Jesus's Resurrection so disturbing to them?

Meditate: Jesus involves angels—messengers of good news who watch and care for us—in his plans. Have you ever experienced that care or guidance from an angel? Offer thanksgiving to God for this protection, or ask the Lord for extra guidance or care from an angel in something you're currently dealing with.

Closing Prayer

Let us pray: O God, let us exult forever in renewed youthfulness of spirit that
we may look forward in confident hope to the rejoicing of the day of Resurrection. Through Jesus Christ, Our Lord. **Amen.**

Second Thursday of Easter

Morning Prayer

Psalm Verse

> Visit the vine and protect it, **the vine your right hand has
> planted.**
>> —Psalm 80:15–16, Liturgy of the Hours translation

Contemplate

Imagine God tending his vine—God's people throughout all ages—and you
on the vine, receiving life-giving nourishment.

*Holy Spirit, allow your divine life to flow in me, to help me be a witness to what
God has done.*

Enter the Word of God

Introduction

Being questioned before the Sanhedrin gives Peter another opportunity to
preach God's plan of salvation to these religious leaders. Peter asserts that
because the apostles are witnesses to the reality that God raised Jesus from the
dead in order to give his Chosen People, Israel, the chance to have their sins
forgiven, they must obey God and not the Sanhedrin, and continue to spread
this Good News.

✳ Scripture Reading: Acts 5:25–33 ✳

Evening Prayer

Verse to Remember

> Jesus was carried up into heaven. **And the disciples worshiped him, and returned to Jerusalem with great joy.**
>
> —cf. Luke 24:51–52

Respond to God's Word

 What truth do you see revealed about each Divine Person—Father, Son, and Spirit—in Peter's response?

 Why did God raise Jesus from the dead and lift him up to his right hand?

 Meditate: Reflect on Jesus's full humanity at God's right hand, interceding for you.

Closing Prayer

Let us pray: O God, let us exult forever in renewed youthfulness of spirit that we may look forward in confident hope to the rejoicing of the day of Resurrection. Through Jesus Christ, Our Lord. **Amen.**

Second Friday of Easter

Morning Prayer

Psalm Verse

> Make me hear joy and gladness; **let the bones which you have broken rejoice.**
>
> —Psalm 51:8

Contemplate

Visualize God bringing refreshment into your soul, to a place you desire healing for.

Lord Jesus, you know the reality of human pain and brokenness, and yet you don't shy away from it—you draw near to us. Help me trust that you will see me through any suffering you allow to happen in my life.

Enter the Word of God

Introduction

As the Sanhedrin decides what to do next with the apostles, a highly respected Pharisee member of the council, Gamaliel, advocates that they simply be let go and left alone to show whether God is truly behind this new movement. The apostles are joyful, recognizing that God is working through them, even amid suffering, to allow his plan to continue.

✳ Scripture Reading: Acts 5:33–42 ✳

Evening Prayer

Verse to Remember

> Jesus was carried up into heaven. **And the disciples worshiped him, and returned to Jerusalem with great joy.**
> —cf. Luke 24:51–52

Respond to God's Word

✎ Which key points in Gamaliel's message stand out to you?

✝ What do Gamaliel's words show about how God guides us, his creations, in his plans?

 Meditate: Where can you ask to cooperate with God's plan more? Ask the Lord for guidance in prayer.

Closing Prayer

Let us pray: O God, let us exult forever in renewed youthfulness of spirit that we may look forward in confident hope to the rejoicing of the day of Resurrection. Through Jesus Christ, Our Lord. **Amen.**

Second Saturday of Easter

Morning Prayer

Psalm Verse

> You have exalted my horn like that of the wild ox; **you have poured over me fresh oil.**
>
> —Psalm 92:10

Contemplate

Imagine God choosing you, in all of your uniqueness, rough edges, and restlessness, to be filled with the Holy Spirit for a specific purpose.

Lord, let the preparation you have begun in me be used for the purposes you desire.

Enter the Word of God

Introduction

As the *ekklesia* (Church) continues to grow in Jerusalem, tensions increase between Jews from different linguistic and cultural backgrounds. Some Hellenists—Jews whose families have lived away from the provinces of Judea and Galilee, and typically speak Greek rather than Hebrew—do live in the city of Jerusalem as a minority group. This leads to a practical problem, which is addressed through a new order of ministry, called *diakonia* (meaning "service," root of the English term *deacon*) to complement the existing *episkope* (office of overseers, bishops).

✴ Scripture Reading: Acts 6:1–7 ✴

Evening Prayer

Verse to Remember

> Jesus was carried up into heaven. **And the disciples worshiped him, and returned to Jerusalem with great joy.**
>
> —cf. Luke 24:51–52

Respond to God's Word

 Find the problem that emerges as the community expands to include both Jews from Judea and Jews from the surrounding Greek areas.

 How is the reality of Jesus's presence with each of his followers seen in the way the community of believers approaches this new problem stemming from their growth?

Meditate: We hear that even a group of Temple priests are becoming believers. What might that conversion have been like for them? Recall a conversion at some point in your life—it might be big or small—and prayerfully reflect on how God led you through that change.

Closing Prayer

Let us pray: O God, let us exult forever in renewed youthfulness of spirit, that we may look forward in confident hope to the rejoicing of the day of Resurrection. Through Jesus Christ, Our Lord. **Amen.**

Third Sunday of Easter

Morning Prayer

Psalm Verse

> Young men and maidens together, old men and children!
> **Let them praise the name of the Lord, for his name alone is exalted.**
>
> —Psalm 148:12–13a

Contemplate

Visualize your place in the Body of Christ, connected to Christ Jesus the Head, the Spirit and praise of the Body filling you.

Christ Jesus, your Body grows to include more and more different people. Protect your Church from division.

Enter the Word of God

Introduction

Just as God has used opposition from certain Jewish religious leaders to bring forth testimonies of praise and opportunities to spread the Gospel, God uses this new situation of conflict within the Church to advance his plan of salvation in new ways. All of the newly ordained deacons have Greek names, a clue that most of them may have been Hellenists or familiar with the Hellenist culture.

✳ Scripture Reading: Acts 6:5–15 ✳

Evening Prayer

Verse to Remember

> You shall receive power **when the Holy Spirit has come upon you.**
>
> —Acts 1:8

Respond to God's Word

What evidence do you see of different reactions within the Jewish community to Jesus's followers? See verses 7, 9, and 12.

Grace is God's divine character present and working in us. In what ways is God perfecting Stephen, making him more like Jesus?

Meditate: Reflect on what it might look like for a follower of Jesus to look or act like an angel. Can you recall a time when you (or another person) experienced what seemed like an angelic intervention? Offer God thanks, or ask God to give you greater protection and care from angels.

Closing Prayer

Let us pray: O God, let us exult forever in renewed youthfulness of spirit that we may look forward in confident hope to the rejoicing of the day of Resurrection. Through Jesus Christ, Our Lord. **Amen.**

Third Monday of Easter

Morning Prayer

Psalm Verse

> Ascribe to the LORD, O families of the peoples, **ascribe to the LORD glory and strength!**
>
> —Psalm 96:7

Contemplate

Focus on God's incredible desire to draw together all men and women, in different places and in different ages, into his family.

God our Father, you are ever on the move to call us, your scattered children, into your family. Give me the energy and desire to lead others into your kingdom.

Enter the Word of God

Introduction

Some of the Hellenist Jews staunchly disagree with Stephen's teaching and arrange for him to be questioned by the Sanhedrin. God uses this situation to give Stephen an opportunity to explain how God's plan has been revealed throughout all of Israel's long history.

✳ Scripture Reading: Acts 6:11–7:53 ✳

Evening Prayer

Verse to Remember

> You shall receive power **when the Holy Spirit has come upon you.**
>
> —Acts 1:8

Respond to God's Word

 Find what the (false) witnesses claim Stephen did. Why are they so upset by this?

† How does Stephen's theme of God moving his people in new directions, despite people rejecting it, relate to the earthly life, death, and Resurrection of Jesus?

Meditate: Call to mind a time when you were moving in a new direction (or perhaps the time is now). How was God leading you? What were your hesitations you could share with Jesus?

Closing Prayer

Let us pray: Almighty, ever-living God, lead us, your humble flock, to follow where our brave Shepherd has gone before. Through Jesus Christ, Our Lord. **Amen.**

Third Tuesday of Easter

Morning Prayer

Psalm Verse

· [May God] make his face to shine upon us, **that your way may be known upon earth, your saving power among all nations.**

—Psalm 67:1b–2

Contemplate

Visualize the Lord Jesus turning his face toward you so that you reflect his light to those around you.

Jesus, let the humanity of your face give me new hope that while I am not God, I have a role to play in God's plan to spread his salvation across the earth.

Enter the Word of God

Introduction

Stephen concludes his interpretation of the Hebrew Scriptures and Israel's journey, showing that God's plan, from Abraham to Moses, was always universal and that the rejection by some "religious insiders" is nothing new. Stephen is stoned by religious vigilantes and dies as Jesus did, offering forgiveness to those who killed him.

✴ Scripture Reading: Acts 7:51–8:1a ✴

Evening Prayer

Verse to Remember

> You shall receive power **when the Holy Spirit has come upon you.**
>
> —Acts 1:8

Respond to God's Word

 For the early Jewish believers, circumcision was an outward sign of God's covenant that changed a person permanently. What does Stephen mean when he tells the high priest and his assembly that their hearts and eyes are uncircumcised?

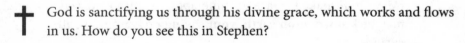 God is sanctifying us through his divine grace, which works and flows in us. How do you see this in Stephen?

Meditate: Baptism unites us with Jesus the Messiah so that we can be made like him through his grace. Ask the Holy Spirit to come into your life now to enable you to become more like Jesus.

Closing Prayer

Let us pray: Almighty, ever-living God, lead us, your humble flock, to follow where our brave Shepherd has gone before. Through Jesus Christ, Our Lord. **Amen.**

Third Wednesday of Easter

Morning Prayer

Psalm Verse

> All the nations you have made shall come and bow down
> before you, O LORD, **and shall glorify your name.**
>
> —Psalm 86:9

Contemplate

Delight in the unbounded energy of the Holy Spirit, who moves conversion
in every person who believes in the Lord.

*God, I am grateful for the movement of your Spirit in me. Thank you for the signs
and nudges that guide me on your path.*

Enter the Word of God

Introduction

Due to threats and violence following the murder of Stephen, many of the
Church in Jerusalem (but not the apostles) are pushed out of the city to the
surrounding regions of Judea and Samaria. Jesus's declaration in Acts 1:8 is
happening in unexpected ways through believers who are not leaders like the
Twelve.

✳ Scripture Reading: Acts 8:1b–25 ✳

Evening Prayer

Verse to Remember

> You shall receive power **when the Holy Spirit has come upon
> you.**
>
> —Acts 1:8

Respond to God's Word

 Find the new locations beyond Jerusalem where the message of God's plan of salvation is now being heard.

How do we see the presence of Jesus in those who believe in him in this passage?

Meditate: The people in Samaria's baptisms are without the Holy Spirit, so they are completed through the laying on of hands. In the Sacrament of Baptism, the Holy Spirit is given fully but can lie dormant at times. Ask for a new release of the Holy Spirit in your life.

Closing Prayer

Let us pray: Almighty, ever-living God, lead us, your humble flock, to follow where our brave Shepherd has gone before. Through Jesus Christ, Our Lord. **Amen.**

Third Thursday of Easter

Morning Prayer

Psalm Verse

> Glorious things are spoken of you, O city of God. **Among those who know me I mention Rahab and Babylon; behold, Philistia and Tyre, with Ethiopia.**
>
> —Psalm 87:3–4a

Contemplate

The city of God is beyond earth yet tugs at every person's soul.

Lord God, plant your seeds in all hearts that wander and are restless. Give each person the boldness to seek and ask for a deeper understanding of you.

Enter the Word of God

Introduction

One of the Hellenist deacons, Philip, continues to find new people with whom to share the Good News of Jesus the Messiah. The Holy Spirit leads Philip step-by-step to experience that even someone who does not conform to Jewish purity laws, like an Ethiopian eunuch,* is included in God's plan to offer salvation to all people.

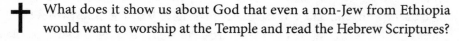

✴ Scripture Reading: Acts 8:26–40 ✴

Evening Prayer

Verse to Remember

> You shall receive power **when the Holy Spirit has come upon you.**
>
> —Acts 1:8

Respond to God's Word

 Find details that reveal the Ethiopian man's background.

✝ What does it show us about God that even a non-Jew from Ethiopia would want to worship at the Temple and read the Hebrew Scriptures?

📿 *Meditate:* The Ethiopian suggests that Philip baptize him. Reflect on a time the Holy Spirit used someone else to draw you to deeper faith in and understanding of God's plan, just as the Ethiopian does for Philip.

Closing Prayer

Let us pray: Almighty, ever-living God, lead us, your humble flock, to follow where our brave Shepherd has gone before. Through Jesus Christ, Our Lord. **Amen.**

Note: * See Deuteronomy 23:2 for the provision in Torah Law that was used to exclude eunuchs from Temple worship. In the ancient world, being made a eunuch was sometimes part of serving in a royal court.

Third Friday of Easter

Morning Prayer

Psalm Verse

> Wash me thoroughly from my iniquity, **and cleanse me from my sin!**
>
> —Psalm 51:2

Contemplate

Consider how perfect and renewing God's ways of washing and cleansing us are.

O God, cleanse from me whatever holds me back from being an active participant, a specially chosen instrument, in your plan unfolding around me.

Enter the Word of God

Introduction

Luke returns to Saul, a young man briefly mentioned in Acts 7:58–8:3. With the permission of the high priest, Saul has been continuing to track down those who believe Jesus is the Messiah, even outside the city of Jerusalem. The Lord visits both Saul and a disciple, Ananias, in visions and intertwines their paths of conversion. As part of the Pharisee movement, Saul has studied the scriptures extensively and is immediately able to start explaining who Jesus truly is in God's plan.

✳ Scripture Reading: Acts 9:1–30 ✳

Evening Prayer

Verse to Remember

> You shall receive power **when the Holy Spirit has come upon you.**
>
> —Acts 1:8

Respond to God's Word

 We learn that the people, mostly Jewish at this point in history, who believed Jesus was the Messiah were called those who belonged to "the Way." Why do you think they were called this?

✝ The voice says to Saul, "Why are you persecuting me?" How is this true? How has Saul been persecuting Jesus?

Meditate: Saul asks, "Who are you, Lord?" This is a foundational question for each of us. Ask, and listen for God to tell you who he is for you personally.

Closing Prayer

Let us pray: Almighty, ever-living God, lead us, your humble flock, to follow where our brave Shepherd has gone before. Through Jesus Christ, Our Lord. **Amen.**

Third Saturday of Easter

Morning Prayer

Psalm Verse

Hear my voice in your steadfast love; **O Lord, in your justice preserve my life.**

—Psalm 119:149

Contemplate

Imagine the Holy Spirit working to raise you up, to preserve you in a place where you feel you are sinking.

O Lord, though I fail, see the good works I do. Sustain me with new life as your faithful servant.

Enter the Word of God

Introduction

Saul comes to Jerusalem and wants to join with the community of believers there. Because they do not trust him, it takes the intervention of Barnabas ("son of encouragement"), who vouches for him, to gain him acceptance. As the Church grows in surrounding areas, Peter and the other apostles continue to lead, guide, and visit the growing number of believers.

✳ Scripture Reading: Acts 9:23–43 ✳

Evening Prayer

Verse to Remember

> You shall receive power **when the Holy Spirit has come upon you.**
>
> —Acts 1:8

Respond to God's Word

 Find some of the characteristics of Tabitha. Why do you think Luke includes them in this scene?

 How does Peter embody the Holy Spirit and Jesus's presence?

Meditate: When Saul tries to join with the believers in Jerusalem, he is first snubbed. Hellenist-Greek Jews even try to kill him, and yet Luke writes that the Church is at peace, even with all the uncertainties of this time. Ask the Lord for peace in your life and in the Church as you experience it.

Closing Prayer

Let us pray: Almighty, ever-living God, lead us, your humble flock, to follow where our brave Shepherd has gone before. Through Jesus Christ, Our Lord. **Amen.**

Fourth Sunday of Easter

Morning Prayer

Psalm Verse

> The stone which the builders rejected has become the cornerstone. **This is the LORD's doing; it is marvelous in our eyes.**
>
> —Psalm 118:22–23

Contemplate

Visualize the Lord doing and moving, as you marvel.

Lord God, your plans always contain surprises. Open my heart to sense and move toward whatever you desire to do in my life.

Enter the Word of God

Introduction

Cornelius is a gentile military officer; he is a believer, but not Jewish. God prepares both Cornelius and Peter through visions for an encounter with one another. Peter is initially confused by his vision but receives external signs that guide him into God's plan, culminating with the stunning sign of Gentiles also being filled with the Holy Spirit, just as Jewish believers had been.

✠ Scripture Reading: Acts 10:1–48 ✠

Evening Prayer

Verse to Remember

> The Lord has risen indeed, **and has appeared to Simon [Peter]!**
>
> —Luke 24:34

Respond to God's Word

 What words show how Peter's entry into Cornelius's home is crossing a religious and/or cultural barrier?

 What does this reveal to us about who the Holy Spirit is and how the Holy Spirit chooses to work?

Meditate: God communicates with both Cornelius and Peter through prayer experiences in which they are confused. Yet external signs after the fact help each man to understand God's message. Has this ever happened to you?

Closing Prayer

Let us pray: Almighty, ever-living God, lead us, your humble flock, to follow where our brave Shepherd has gone before. Through Jesus Christ, Our Lord. **Amen.**

Fourth Monday of Easter

Morning Prayer

Psalm Verse

> Let the favor of the Lord our God be upon us, **and establish the work of our hands upon us.**
>
> —Psalm 90:17a

Contemplate

Envision how God can take your work, your efforts, and your passions and infuse them with his grace.

Lord our God, give me the energy to work toward good in my life and the trust that you are truly in control.

Enter the Word of God

Introduction

News about what Peter and his companions have done at Cornelius's house spreads, and not everyone is pleased! After receiving criticism for his actions, Peter responds by explaining what happened and how God led him and some disciples to extend baptism to the Gentiles.

✼ Scripture Reading: Acts 11:1–18 ✼

Evening Prayer

Verse to Remember

> The Lord has risen indeed, **and has appeared to Simon [Peter]!**
>
> —Luke 24:34

Respond to God's Word

 Find words that reveal why the believers in Judea question Peter.

✝ God's eternal plan is to unite all people to him, in his family. How does God gradually go about doing this?

🕯 *Meditate:* What characteristics of Peter make him able to cooperate with God's plan as it unfolds? Ask for the virtues and spiritual gifts you need to cooperate more as a part of God's plan of salvation for others.

Closing Prayer

Let us pray: Lord God, help us, your children, bear much fruit under your protective care. Through Jesus Christ, Our Lord. **Amen.**

Fourth Tuesday of Easter

Morning Prayer

Psalm Verse

> Incline your ear to me; **answer me speedily in the day when I call!**
>
> —Psalm 102:2b

Contemplate

Imagine God leaning in toward you when situations seem most uncertain.

Holy Spirit, you are our guide, the one who gives us words of truth when we most need it. Allow me to hear you when I need it the most.

Enter the Word of God

Introduction

Luke brings us back to a previous storyline, providing an update on the Jewish believers, many of whom were Hellenist Jews who were driven from their homes and scattered after Stephen was martyred. These ordinary believers have been telling first fellow Jews and then Gentiles who Jesus is. The community of believers is growing and spreading out geographically yet remains one in Christ, united through leadership, teaching, and sharing of resources.

 **✳ Scripture Reading: Acts 11:19–30 ✳**

Evening Prayer

Verse to Remember

> The Lord has risen indeed, **and has appeared to Simon [Peter]!**

Respond to God's Word

 Look back at Acts 8:1. How would you describe the people who were scattered because of the persecution? What do you think they told people in these new places?

How do we see God's plan to reveal himself to the people called "Israel" first, and then through Israel as a light to all others, unfolding?

Meditate: Place yourself in the position of the people who were scattered. You have no *Catechism,* no written New Testament, and no books on the Catholic faith. What would you tell people based on your life experience to convince them to turn to the Lord? Spend time in prayer pondering what leads you to believe that God's plan is real.

Closing Prayer

Let us pray: Lord God, help us, your children, bear much fruit under your protective care. Through Jesus Christ, Our Lord. **Amen.**

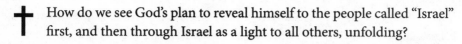

Fourth Wednesday of Easter

Morning Prayer

Psalm Verse

> Put not your trust in princes, in a son of man, in whom there is no help. **When his breath departs, he returns to his earth; on that very day his plans perish.**
> —Psalm 146:3–4

Contemplate

Bask in the infinite eternity of God: Creator, King, and Lover of the universe.

Almighty and eternal God, let my heart desire you and not be harmed or dismayed by trusting in material things or earthly power.

Enter the Word of God

Introduction

Luke calls our attention to how God's plan unfolds amid transitions within human history.* James (one of the sons of Zebedee) becomes the first of the Twelve to be martyred. A different James becomes the leader of the Church in Jerusalem as Peter begins to minister elsewhere. King Herod and his evil come to their earthly end. Even when human events bring opposition or obstacles, the Holy Spirit is still guiding and accompanying God's people, fostering not just growth through addition but growth by multiplication.

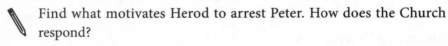 Scripture Reading: Acts 12:1–25 ✷

Evening Prayer

Verse to Remember

> The Lord has risen indeed, **and has appeared to Simon [Peter]!**
>
>   —Luke 24:34

Respond to God's Word

✎ Find what motivates Herod to arrest Peter. How does the Church respond?

✝ How does the example of King Herod give us a glimpse of the justice God will enact when he brings all things to fulfillment in the Second Coming of Christ?

🕯 *Meditate:* Ask the Lord in what ways he wants his Word to grow and multiply (see verse 24) in your life, even amid the chaos and disturbance of Herod-like forces?

Closing Prayer

Let us pray: Lord God, help us, your children, bear much fruit under your protective care. Through Jesus Christ, Our Lord. **Amen.**

Note: * For example, at the start of Luke's gospel, Caesar Augustus's decree for a census causes Joseph and Mary to travel to Bethlehem (see Lk 2:1–2).

Fourth Thursday of Easter

Morning Prayer

Psalm Verse

> Teach me to do your will, for you are my God! **Let your good spirit lead me on a level path!**
>
> —Psalm 143:10

Contemplate

God has a path for you and sends his Holy Spirit to lead you on it.

God our Father, you know me and care about everything I do. Allow me to walk more trustfully on the path you are slowly revealing to me.

Enter the Word of God

Introduction

Saul and Barnabas return to Antioch after their trip to Jerusalem. Many of the ways we pray today, such as through communal gatherings, fasting, and the use of hand gestures, are present in this glimpse of the early church.

✳ Scripture Reading: Acts 12:24–13:5 ✳

Evening Prayer

Verse to Remember

> The Lord has risen indeed, **and has appeared to Simon [Peter]!**
>
> —Luke 24:34

Respond to God's Word

What jumps out at you in this passage today?

✝ Some of the named believers in Antioch serve as prophets and teachers. In baptism, anointing with sacred chrism signifies the participation of the baptized in the Messiah's kingly (to include teaching) and prophetic roles (see *CCC*, 1291). What does our participation in Jesus's roles reveal about us?

🕯 *Meditate:* The church in Antioch worships and fasts as part of their process of discernment. Ask the Holy Spirit to guide you in uniting your worship and practices as a Catholic Christian with the difficult decisions you may face.

Closing Prayer

Let us pray: Lord God, help us, your children, bear much fruit under your protective care. Through Jesus Christ, Our Lord. **Amen.**

Fourth Friday of Easter

Morning Prayer

Psalm Verse

> He makes peace in your borders; **he fills you with the finest of the wheat.**
>
> —Psalm 147:14

Contemplate

Imagine God tending and cultivating the places and spaces where you live your life as one would tend a garden.

Lord God, help me rest from my own labors and look for the places where your Spirit is moving, offering peace, consolation, and satisfaction.

Enter the Word of God

Introduction

Barnabas and Saul (now also noted as Paul; see verse 9) begin their journey of missionary outreach, teaching their fellow Jews that Jesus is the Savior that God had prepared them for in the Hebrew Scriptures.

✠ Scripture Reading: Acts 13:5–41 ✠

Evening Prayer

Verse to Remember

> The Lord has risen indeed, **and has appeared to Simon [Peter]!**
>
> —Luke 24:34

Respond to God's Word

When Paul, Barnabas, and John Mark arrive in a city, where do they go first to announce God's plan of salvation? See verses 5 and 14.

How is Jesus the fulfillment of what God has always promised to his people? See verses 32–33 and 38–39.

Meditate: Paul warns the people who hear him preach not to doubt that God is really acting and working in history right now. Where might you be called to see God at work in your life?

Closing Prayer

Let us pray: Lord God, help us, your children, bear much fruit under your protective care. Through Jesus Christ, Our Lord. **Amen.**

Fourth Saturday of Easter

Morning Prayer

Psalm Verse

> For you, O Lord, have made me glad by your work; **at the works of your hands I sing for joy.**
>
> —Psalm 92:4

Contemplate

Think of God, who gives you joy—no matter how small or large, how hidden or shared.

Lord, fill me with your divine gift of joy as I open my eyes anew to how you are working in and around me.

Enter the Word of God

Introduction

As Jesus experienced during his earthly ministry in Galilee, God's message always seems to have a mixed response. Many Jews do believe that Jesus is the Messiah, but some are jealous or oppose the message for other reasons. Paul and Barnabas understand the prophet Isaiah's words to be a foreshadowing of Israel's ultimate destiny as a light bringing salvation to all people.

✳ Scripture Reading: Acts 13:42–52 ✳

Evening Prayer

Verse to Remember

> The Lord has risen indeed, **and has appeared to Simon [Peter]!**
>
> —Luke 24:34

Respond to God's Word

 Find some of the reactions of people, both Gentiles and Jews, who hear Paul preach at the synagogue.

 How is Isaiah's prophecy (see verse 47) being fulfilled in these years described in Acts?

 Meditate: Verses 46 and 48 mention eternal life, a new age of living in Jesus the Christ. What distinguishes this new life, in your personal experience?

Closing Prayer

Let us pray: Lord God, help us, your children, bear much fruit under your protective care. Through Jesus Christ, Our Lord. **Amen.**

Fifth Sunday of Easter

Morning Prayer

Psalm Verse

> Praise the LORD! **Sing to the Lord a new song, his praise in the assembly of the faithful!**
>
> —Psalm 149:1

Contemplate

Try to hear the new song God is singing into the world, through his people, the Body of Christ.

God our Father, hear and welcome the new song, the new praises, I give to you today in my words and deeds.

Enter the Word of God

Introduction

Filled with the Holy Spirit and with joy, Barnabas and Paul continue their journey into new territory despite obstacles. Sometimes a positive outcome of their evangelism results in misunderstanding and a bit of chaos! Some Jews from Antioch who oppose their message arrive and rally others to attack and drive Paul out of the city of Lystra.

✴ Scripture Reading: Acts 13:51–14:20 ✴

Evening Prayer

Verse to Remember

> [The Holy Spirit] will teach you all things, **and bring to your remembrance all that I have said to you.**
>
> —John 14:26

Respond to God's Word

 What do you notice about Paul, Barnabas, and John Mark's ministry in Iconium that has happened before?

✝ How does Paul explain that God was at work, patiently unveiling his plan, even before Jesus was incarnate? See Mark 14:16–17.

🕯 *Meditate:* Does Mark 13:52 surprise you, given what is happening? How can you ask for joy and more of the Holy Spirit despite uncertainty and the ups and downs in your day-to-day life?

Closing Prayer

Let us pray: Lord God, help us, your children, bear much fruit under your protective care. Through Jesus Christ, Our Lord. **Amen.**

Fifth Monday of Easter

Morning Prayer

Psalm Verse

> May the LORD give strength to his people! **May the LORD bless his people with peace!**
>
> —Psalm 29:11

Contemplate

God loves you as an individual, but also calls you as one of his people to be supported and strengthened in Christ's Body.

Christ Jesus, head of your Body, allow me to both give and receive your blessings within your Body.

Enter the Word of God

Introduction

Paul and Barnabas return to their earlier mission stops to continue to form the faith of the new believers and appoint "elders" (*presbyteroi* in Greek, the root of *priest*) to continue to shepherd and govern the growing Church, along with the bishops (*episkopoi*) and deacons (*deaconoi*) already seen.

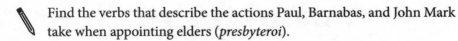 Scripture Reading: Acts 14:19–28 ✸

Evening Prayer

Verse to Remember

> [The Holy Spirit] will teach you all things, **and bring to your remembrance all that I have said to you.**
>
> —John 14:26

Respond to God's Word

Find the verbs that describe the actions Paul, Barnabas, and John Mark take when appointing elders (*presbyteroi*).

How does suffering enable us to experience the kingdom of God in new, different, or unexpected ways? See verse 22.

Meditate: Reflect in prayer on all the things God has done in your life and the doors he has opened up (see verse 27).

Closing Prayer

Let us pray: Grant, almighty God, that what we relive in remembrance of this Easter season, we may always hold to in what we say and do. Through Jesus Christ, Our Lord. **Amen.**

Fifth Tuesday of Easter

Morning Prayer

Psalm Verse

> The counsel of the LORD stands for ever, **the thoughts of his heart to all generations.**
>
> —Psalm 33:11

Contemplate

Allow the counsel of the Lord to fill you.

Holy Spirit, you are our Counselor, our Advocate; come to my aid, and lead me into good choices that resonate for generations.

Enter the Word of God

Introduction

Paul and Barnabas are back in Antioch, visiting with the believers who first prayed over them and sent them on a mission. However, some believers from the province of Judea arrive and start teaching the community that one must be circumcised to be saved. There is such controversy and confusion over this issue that the apostles and elders (priests) convene a council in Jerusalem to discern God's will for the Church.

✴ Scripture Reading: Acts 15:1–6 ✴

Evening Prayer

Verse to Remember

> [The Holy Spirit] will teach you all things, **and bring to your remembrance all that I have said to you.**
>
> —John 14:26

Respond to God's Word

 What stands out to you in this passage?

✝ How does the way the Church begins to address this disagreement reveal the Church as the Body of Christ?

🕯 *Meditate:* When have you ever been tempted to think, "I cannot be saved unless I do such-and-such work"? How does your faith in Jesus as Savior and rescuer give you confidence that Jesus's grace, and not your works, is what is essential for experiencing eternal life?

Closing Prayer

Let us pray: Grant, almighty God, that what we relive in remembrance of this Easter season, we may always hold to in what we say and do. Through Jesus Christ, Our Lord. **Amen.**

Fifth Wednesday of Easter

Morning Prayer

Psalm Verse

> For with you is the fountain of life; **in your light do we see light.**
>
> —Psalm 36:9

Contemplate

Imagine the light of God—the brightness, the warmth—changing the way you see a situation or yourself.

Lord Jesus, you are light from light. Allow me to see the world today in your light.

Enter the Word of God

Introduction

Through a council, the Church sets out to address an issue that has been causing division among believers. The council of leaders in Jerusalem looks at the evidence of both signs and God's revelation, examining the recent experiences of Jesus's followers through the lens of the Hebrew Scriptures they know as God's Word.

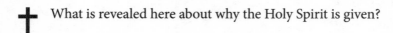

✳ Scripture Reading: Acts 15:6–21 ✳

Evening Prayer

Verse to Remember

> [The Holy Spirit] will teach you all things, **and bring to your remembrance all that I have said to you.**
>
> —John 14:26

Respond to God's Word

 What do you think Peter's main point is in verse 10?

✝ What is revealed here about why the Holy Spirit is given?

🕯 *Meditate:* To decide how to resolve this divisive dispute, the apostles and elders gathered together to debate and share their experiences of God working, and compare this to God's revelation in the sacred scriptures. How can you use this method of discernment in your own life?

Closing Prayer

Let us pray: Grant, almighty God, that what we relive in remembrance of this Easter season, we may always hold to in what we say and do. Through Jesus Christ, Our Lord. **Amen.**

Fifth Thursday of Easter

Morning Prayer

Psalm Verse

> Your praise reaches to the ends of the earth. **Your right hand is filled with victory.**
>
> —Psalm 48:10

Contemplate

Luxuriate in the love of the Holy Spirit, which extends God's message to the ends of the earth and to every part of your inner being.

Come, Holy Spirit, and bring God's message to the places and people in the world most in need of consolation.

Enter the Word of God

Introduction

Following the will of the Holy Spirit, the council makes a decision and takes practical steps to communicate it with the entire Church through sending out letters with people who can explain the decision. Reassured that they are not veering from Church teaching, Paul and Barnabas begin to plan another missionary journey but get in an argument about whom to include on the missionary team.

✸ Scripture Reading: Acts 15:19–41 ✸

Evening Prayer

Verse to Remember

> [The Holy Spirit] will teach you all things, **and bring to your remembrance all that I have said to you.**
>
> —John 14:26

Respond to God's Word

 Find a method the apostles and elders plan to use to communicate their decision to the Church.

 What does verse 28 show about God's continuing plan for the Church?

 Meditate: Paul and Barnabas have been through so much together, yet they decide to separate because of a dispute over John Mark. Both Barnabas and Paul continue to serve the Church and God, not losing faith in God's plan. How can you be strengthened by their very human example?

Closing Prayer

Let us pray: Grant, almighty God, that what we relive in remembrance of this Easter season, we may always hold to in what we say and do. Through Jesus Christ, Our Lord. **Amen.**

Fifth Friday of Easter

Morning Prayer

Psalm Verse

> Make a joyful noise to the LORD, all the lands! **Serve the Lord with gladness! Come into his presence with singing!**
> —Psalm 100:1–2

Contemplate

In the Body of Christ, even while here on earth, you are connected to Jesus the Head, in his presence with all of his saints throughout all ages and all places. Soak in this presence.

Jesus, Son of God, strengthen my bonds with your Body and nourish my relationships with others.

Enter the Word of God

Introduction

Paul and his coworkers (fellow missionaries) leave Antioch on a journey throughout the Aegean Sea area to teach and encourage believers while always being ready to share the Good News with those who have not yet heard or believed it. Paul asks Timothy, a believer with parents from different ethnic/ religious backgrounds, to join him in the ministry.

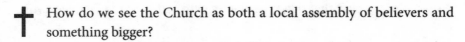 Scripture Reading: Acts 16:1–10

Evening Prayer

Verse to Remember

> [The Holy Spirit] will teach you all things, **and bring to your remembrance all that I have said to you.**
>
> —John 14:26

Respond to God's Word

 Find how Paul and Timothy play a role in spreading the decision reached in Jerusalem.

✝ How do we see the Church as both a local assembly of believers and something bigger?

☐ *Meditate:* In verse 6 we hear of the Holy Spirit preventing or stopping Paul and Timothy from doing something. Have you ever experienced a "no" from the Lord in prayer? Ask God where you can be more open to the "no" of the Holy Spirit.

Closing Prayer

Let us pray: Grant, almighty God, that what we relive in remembrance of this Easter season, we may always hold to in what we say and do. Through Jesus Christ, Our Lord. **Amen.**

Fifth Saturday of Easter

Morning Prayer

Psalm Verse

> But you are near, O LORD, **and all your commandments are**
> **true.**
>
> —Psalm 119:151

Contemplate

Feel the nearness and closeness of Jesus, true God and true man, your brother
and friend.

Lord God, I praise you, for wherever I go, you are there, guiding me in whatever
new or unexpected circumstances I face.

Enter the Word of God

Introduction

Paul and his team have a flexible plan and go where the Holy Spirit prompts
or opens doors for them. In Philippi (their first stop outside of Asia), there
are so few Jews (not even a synagogue, just an informal place of prayer on the
outskirts of the city) that they share God's plan with a woman named Lydia.

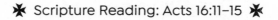 Scripture Reading: Acts 16:11–15 ✖

Evening Prayer

Verse to Remember

> [The Holy Spirit] will teach you all things, **and bring to your**
> **remembrance all that I have said to you.**
>
> —John 14:26

Respond to God's Word

 Notice the use of "we" starting in verse 11. What does this show us about the relationship between Luke, the human author of Acts, and Paul?

What does it reveal to us about the Sacrament of Baptism that Lydia and her entire household, who have just begun to believe in Jesus as Savior, immediately receive baptism?

Meditate: Pray for the Holy Spirit to help your heart pay attention, to be open to how God might be speaking—even through other people, as Lydia demonstrates in verse 14.

Closing Prayer

Let us pray: Grant, almighty God, that what we relive in remembrance of this Easter season, we may always hold to in what we say and do. Through Jesus Christ, Our Lord. **Amen.**

Sixth Sunday of Easter

Morning Prayer

Psalm Verse

Let everything that breathes praise the LORD! **Praise the LORD!**

—Psalm 150:6

Contemplate

Our existence as humanity is breathed into us by God's breath, the Holy Spirit. Contemplate God's Spirit filling you and leaving you as you breathe naturally for a few moments.

Holy Spirit, you are the giver of life; flow into and through me, rejuvenate me, relax me, and sustain me today.

Enter the Word of God

Introduction

Philippi is a Roman colony-city in an ethnically Greek land. The Romans are concerned about what these Jews, Paul and Silas, are promoting and jail them. This leads to another prison release tied to intercessory prayer (see also Acts 5:19–21, 12:6–11)! Against all odds, a local Church—founded on the testimonies and convictions of a businesswoman and a jailer, rather than any Jewish religious leaders—begins to grow in Philippi.

✳ Scripture Reading: Acts 16:16–40 ✳

Evening Prayer

Verse to Remember

> And they were all filled with the Holy Spirit. **And proclaimed the mighty works of God.**
>
> —cf. Acts 2:4, 11

Respond to God's Word

 What is the cause of Paul and Silas's arrest? See verses 19–21.

 What truths about Jesus do you think they spoke?

Meditate: When do you remember first doing what Paul and Silas encourage in verse 31: having a belief in the Lord that will save you? If you cannot remember it, be intentional and open right now with Jesus and tell him that you do believe he saved you through his death on the Cross and his Resurrection and is saving you now.

Closing Prayer

Let us pray: Grant, almighty God, that what we relive in remembrance of this Easter season, we may always hold to in what we say and do. Through Jesus Christ, Our Lord. **Amen.**

Sixth Monday of Easter

Morning Prayer

Psalm Verse

> Day to day pours forth speech, **and night to night declares knowledge.**
>
> —Psalm 19:2

Contemplate

The Holy Spirit is known as the giver of truth. Open your heart, and allow God's truth to penetrate you deeply.

Holy Spirit, guide my words and mind so that I will speak, listen, and understand others in the way you desire.

Enter the Word of God

Introduction

Paul and his missionary team continue west into Greece, reaching Thessalonica and Beroea, two cities with established Jewish synagogues. Paul teaches God's plan of salvation, and as usual, God's plan is not accepted by all, but some Jews and some Gentiles do respond with faith and believe in Jesus as Lord.

✳ Scripture Reading: Acts 17:1–15 ✳

Evening Prayer

Verse to Remember

> And they were all filled with the Holy Spirit. **And proclaimed the mighty works of God.**
>
> —cf. Acts 2:4, 11

Respond to God's Word

 Find who responds positively to Paul and Silas's message at the synagogues.

 How is the declaration that Jesus is the Son of God, the one who can forgive sins, the one who can open the kingdom of God, something that disrupts the world?

 Meditate: When do you feel most eager, interested, and willing to search the scriptures? Ask the Lord for more gifts to bring you to a deeper understanding of his Word.

Closing Prayer

Let us pray: Graciously hear our prayers, O God, so that we may experience, as Jesus promised, his abiding presence among us until the end of the world. Through Jesus Christ, Our Lord. **Amen.**

Sixth Tuesday of Easter

Morning Prayer

Psalm Verse

> You visit the earth and water it, **you greatly enrich it.**
> —Psalm 65:9

Contemplate

Consider God's protective care and enrichment of all the earth and all people, even those who do not yet know him by name. Embrace this love in your soul.

Come, Holy Spirit, refresh me for the mission to which you have called me.

Enter the Word of God

Introduction

Continuing south down the peninsula to Athens, Paul keeps adjusting to the reality around him and shows yet another way to announce the Gospel (*evangel*, the root word of *evangelization*). He goes to the Areopagus (or Mars Hill), a site dedicated to a pagan "god," and praises the religious efforts of the Greeks. Paul doesn't use the name of Jesus in this speech and even quotes a Greek philosopher-poet to explain God's plan. Some who do not believe are still interested enough to want to hear more about God at a later time.

✴ Scripture Reading: Acts 17:16–34 ✴

Evening Prayer

Verse to Remember

> And they were all filled with the Holy Spirit. **And proclaimed the mighty works of God.**
>
> —cf. Acts 2:4, 11

Respond to God's Word

 Imagine you are a first-century Jewish follower of Jesus. What might you think about Paul speaking at a place of pagan religious worship?

 Paul does not speak of Jesus by name in his speech. What truths does he emphasize about God's plan when speaking to this pagan audience?

 Meditate: Paul makes a connection with his pagan audience by praising their religious devotion. Ask the Lord how you can build connections of trust with those who are not believers.

Closing Prayer

Let us pray: Graciously hear our prayers, O God, so that we may experience, as Jesus promised, his abiding presence among us until the end of the world. Through Jesus Christ, Our Lord. **Amen.**

Sixth Wednesday of Easter

Morning Prayer

Psalm Verse

> Light dawns for the righteous, **and joy for the upright in heart.**
>
> —Psalm 97:11

Contemplate

Imagine God revealing his ways and actions in your life slowly, like the dawn, becoming brighter and brighter.

Lord God, I offer you my hopes, actions, and words to come this day, that through your light I will find joy in you, even in surprising places.

Enter the Word of God

Introduction

Paul moves farther south to the booming port city of Corinth, where he continues to reach out to both Gentiles and his fellow Jews. Paul seeks out fellowship with other believers, a married couple named Priscilla and Aquila.

✳ Scripture Reading: Acts 18:1–8 ✳

Evening Prayer

Verse to Remember

> And they were all filled with the Holy Spirit. **And proclaimed the mighty works of God.**
>
> —cf. Acts 2:4, 11

Respond to God's Word

Why do you think Paul makes connections with people like Priscilla, Aquila, and Titius Justus?

How is Paul's shift to focusing on a mission to the Gentiles part of God's plan to "call together all men, scattered and divided by sin, into the unity of his family, the Church" (see *CCC*, 1)?

Meditate: Even after Paul moves on from the Corinth synagogue, Crispus, the ruler of the synagogue, becomes a believer. God never gives up on any of us! Where do you see God's perseverance, God's steady desire to draw close to you, in your life?

Closing Prayer

Let us pray: Graciously hear our prayers, O God, so that we may experience, as Jesus promised, his abiding presence among us until the end of the world. Through Jesus Christ, Our Lord. **Amen.**

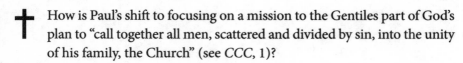

Sixth Thursday of Easter

Morning Prayer

Psalm Verse

> I am the Lord your God, who brought you up out of the land of Egypt. **Open your mouth wide, and I will fill it.**
> —Psalm 81:10

Contemplate

God has been slowly leading us, his family, out of darkness and captivity into a new freedom—his Promised Land—for thousands of years. Contemplate God's loving desire to feed, nurture, and sustain us, slowly.

God our Father, let me open my mind, mouth, and heart to consume and be transformed by your presence.

Enter the Word of God

Introduction

After eighteen months in Corinth, Paul moves on with Priscilla and Aquila to continue to bear witness to Jesus the Messiah in synagogues and nourish the faith of other disciples back in Asia.*

✳ Scripture Reading: Acts 18:9–23 ✳

Evening Prayer

Verse to Remember

> And they were all filled with the Holy Spirit. **And proclaimed the mighty works of God.**
>
> —cf. Acts 2:4, 11

Respond to God's Word

 Use a map to find some of the locations mentioned in this passage (a reading that covers a time span of more than one year).

✝ Why would others claim that Paul was teaching people to worship God the wrong way? See verses 12–13. What did Jesus reveal about the right way to worship God?

Meditate: The idea of the Lord reaching out to you in a vision at night can sound spectacular or far-fetched, but it does not have to be. God wants to communicate with us in whatever way works. This can include dreams, images, signs, or particular words. Reflect on the ways God communicates with you.

Closing Prayer

Let us pray: Graciously hear our prayers, O God, so that we may experience, as Jesus promised, his abiding presence among us until the end of the world. Through Jesus Christ, Our Lord. **Amen.**

Note: * *Followers of Jesus, believers, brethren,* and *brothers and sisters* are all synonyms for *disciples.* See the Disciples, Apostles, and the Twelve Diagram on page 160.

Sixth Friday of Easter

Morning Prayer

Psalm Verse

> [The LORD] declares his word to Jacob, **his statutes and ordinances to Israel.**
>
> —Psalm 147:19

Contemplate

Listen for God speaking to you, informing both your heart and mind of his truth.

God of truth, sometimes it is a blessing to know your truth, and other times it seems burdensome or confusing. Encourage me in seeking your wisdom and sharing it with others.

Enter the Word of God

Introduction

With Paul continuing to a different location, Priscilla and Aquila stay in Ephesus and meet Apollos, another Jewish believer, from Egypt. Even though Apollos has already come to believe in Jesus as Messiah and has even started to spread the Good News, there is still fruitfulness for him in growing deeper in understanding God's plan. Aquila and Priscilla respond by teaching him.*

✸ Scripture Reading: Acts 18:24–28 ✸

Note: * Paul later calls Priscilla and Aquila his "fellow workers" or "coworkers," showing that this work of mission and ministry is not restricted to an elite few but the mission of all disciples (see Rom 16:3; CCC, 863).

Evening Prayer

Verse to Remember

> And they were all filled with the Holy Spirit. **And proclaimed the mighty works of God.**
>
> —cf. Acts 2:4, 11

Respond to God's Word

 How might you explain the difference between the baptism of John and the baptism of Jesus? See Acts 8:14–17.

 One of the many names for the Church is the "People of God" (see *CCC*, 781–786). How do we see that reality in Apollos, Priscilla, and Aquila?

Meditate: By writing letters to the believers in Achaia, the Christians in Ephesus help Apollos use his gifts for the good of others. Have you ever been called into service, into ministry, or to do something for the good of others due to encouragement? Pray in thanksgiving for the people who have been encouragers in your life.

Closing Prayer

Let us pray: Graciously hear our prayers, O God, so that we may experience, as Jesus promised, his abiding presence among us until the end of the world. Through Jesus Christ, Our Lord. **Amen.**

Sixth Saturday of Easter

Morning Prayer

Psalm Verse

> How great are your works, O Lord! **Your thoughts are very deep!**
>
> —Psalm 92:5

Contemplate

Consider the depth of God's unique plan for your life. Rest comfortably knowing that while the depths of that plan cannot yet be seen, God knows it.

Lord God, day-to-day life can have twists and turns that seem to follow no clear course. Give me the courage to trust in your goodness and that you know me and are leading me closer to you.

Enter the Word of God

Introduction

The believers in Ephesus support Apollos in his desire to continue ministry in Corinth, writing him a letter of recommendation. After Apollos leaves, Paul arrives back in Ephesus and discovers that some in Ephesus identify as disciples of Jesus but have not heard of, or received, the Holy Spirit.

✳ Scripture Reading: Acts 19:1–8 ✳

Evening Prayer

Verse to Remember

> And they were all filled with the Holy Spirit. **And proclaimed the mighty works of God.**
>
> —cf. Acts 2:4, 11

Respond to God's Word

 Imagine how the disciples at Ephesus might have first heard about Jesus and become believers before Paul even arrived.

✝ What are the signs and gestures of the Holy Spirit coming upon believers in this scene?

Meditate: How is the Holy Spirit working in your life? Is the Spirit dormant, meaning you received it in the Sacrament of Baptism but do not have a relationship with the Spirit as you do with God the Father and Jesus, God's Son? Ask the Holy Spirit to come into your heart and soak you, saturate your life so that you see the world with the guidance of the Spirit and the unique spiritual gifts the Spirit desires to give to you.

Closing Prayer

Let us pray: Graciously hear our prayers, O God, so that we may experience, as Jesus promised, his abiding presence among us until the end of the world. Through Jesus Christ, Our Lord. **Amen.**

Seventh Sunday of Easter

Morning Prayer

Psalm Verse

> The LORD reigns; he is robed in majesty; **the LORD is robed, he is girded with strength.**
>
> —Psalm 93:1a

Contemplate

Visualize the Lord's strength as the father of a diverse family of imperfect people across history, including you now.

God Almighty, you reign over the universe even when we do not see it. Touch the situations in my life where I need your strength.

Enter the Word of God

Introduction

Paul demonstrates a personal relationship with the Holy Spirit that affects his daily life. Healings and conversions at his hands* have a negative impact on the local businesses in Ephesus that profit from those participating in pagan worship, leading to a riot and controversy.

✠ Scripture Reading: Acts 19:8–41 ✠

Note: * Even through relics! See Acts 19:12.

Evening Prayer

Verse to Remember

> Go, [Ananias,] for this man [Paul] is a chosen instrument of mine **to carry my name before Gentiles, kings, and Israelites.**
>
> —Acts 9:15, NABRE

Respond to God's Word

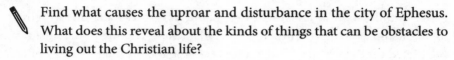 Find what causes the uproar and disturbance in the city of Ephesus. What does this reveal about the kinds of things that can be obstacles to living out the Christian life?

Recall that the early church thought of themselves as belonging to "the Way." What additional ideas do you have as to why the believers called themselves this?

Meditate: Ask the Lord to help you maintain peace and goodwill toward others amid the many seemingly nonspiritual things that can be challenges in our walk as disciples.

Closing Prayer

Let us pray: Graciously hear our prayers, O God, so that we may experience, as Jesus promised, his abiding presence among us until the end of the world. Through Jesus Christ, Our Lord. **Amen.**

Seventh Monday of Easter

Morning Prayer

Psalm Verse

> Blessed are those who dwell in your house, **ever singing your praise!**
>
> —Psalm 84:4

Contemplate

Allow yourself to stop, slow down, and dwell in God's house—God's eternal life shared with you right now.

God our Father, let me experience the blessing anew of the many ways I can enter and encounter your house in my life.

Enter the Word of God

Introduction

Paul continues to form Jesus's followers in the faith and spend time with them in fellowship as a community. The Eucharist (the "breaking of the bread") is celebrated on the first day of the week, echoing the original first day of creation and Jesus's Resurrection day of *new* creation. Paul begins preparations for traveling to Jerusalem.

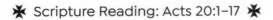 ✳ Scripture Reading: Acts 20:1–17 ✳

Evening Prayer

Verse to Remember

> Go, [Ananias,] for this man [Paul] is a chosen instrument of mine **to carry my name before Gentiles, kings, and Israelites.**
>
> —Acts 9:15, NABRE

Respond to God's Word

 Why is Paul now heading to Jerusalem? See verse 16.

✝ The Eucharist is also called the "breaking of the bread" because this describes one of Jesus's essential actions when he celebrated the Passover (Last Supper) with the Twelve. What spiritual meanings do you find in this term?

⌇ *Meditate:* Paul and the disciples in Troas engage in a long discussion, showing that God's plan in Jesus the Messiah is unfathomably deep!

Allow your prayer to be more conversational; ask the Lord to speak to you through thoughts, writings, and images about something you desire to understand more.

Closing Prayer

Let us pray: O God, grant that from out of the scattered nations, the confusion of many tongues may be gathered by heavenly grace into one great confession of your name. Through Jesus Christ, Our Lord. **Amen.**

Seventh Tuesday of Easter

Morning Prayer

Psalm Verse

Let me hear what God the LORD will speak, **for he will speak peace to his people, to his saints, to those who turn to him in their hearts.**

—Psalm 85:8

Contemplate

Turn your heart to God and receive his peace.

Lord God, you have directed turns in my life that have led me to you, to abiding within you. Thank you for these gifts of conversion.

Enter the Word of God

Introduction

Paul gives a farewell speech of encouragement and teaching to the elders of Ephesus, beginning by reviewing parts of his personal testimony and ministry with them.

✳ Scripture Reading: Acts 20:17–27 ✳

Evening Prayer

Verse to Remember

> Go, [Ananias,] for this man [Paul] is a chosen instrument of mine **to carry my name before Gentiles, kings, and Israelites.**
>
> —Acts 9:15, NABRE

Respond to God's Word

 What resonates with you about how Paul summarizes his style of ministry and witness?

† "The term 'Spirit' translates the Hebrew word *ruah*, which, in its primary sense, means breath, air, wind" (*CCC*, 691). This reminds us that the Holy Spirit can communicate with us through nudges and promptings. How do we see this active in Paul's life?

Meditate: Despite the many things that Paul might find incomplete or still "works in progress," he has peace with his faith in God and with his actions. Ask the Lord to show you where he might be calling you to have peace with yourself and with what is within your realm of influence.

Closing Prayer

Let us pray: O God, grant that from out of the scattered nations, the confusion of many tongues may be gathered by heavenly grace into one great confession of your name. Through Jesus Christ, Our Lord. **Amen.**

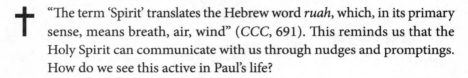

Seventh Wednesday of Easter

Morning Prayer

Psalm Verse

> For great is your merciful love toward me; **you have delivered my soul from the depths of Sheol.**
>
> —Psalm 86:13

Contemplate

Imagine God rescuing you from sinking down.

Lord God, the moment I accepted your great rescue and allowed your mercy to overflow my soul, I began a new relationship with you. Thank you for continuing to sustain me on the path of life.

Enter the Word of God

Introduction

Paul continues his farewell message in Ephesus, preparing the Church's leaders for struggles that will come and reminding them of the importance of always drawing close to God in prayer.

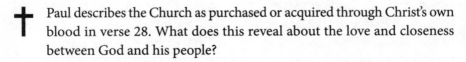 Scripture Reading: Acts 20:28–38 ✴

Evening Prayer

Verse to Remember

> Go, [Ananias,] for this man [Paul] is a chosen instrument
> of mine **to carry my name before Gentiles, kings, and
> Israelites.**
> —Acts 9:15, NABRE

Respond to God's Word

 How would you describe the tone or mood of this final farewell?

✝ Paul describes the Church as purchased or acquired through Christ's own blood in verse 28. What does this reveal about the love and closeness between God and his people?

Meditate: Paul entrusts the elders here in Miletus to the gracious Word of God, which builds us up and provides an inheritance, meaning the riches of a family passed on to children. Reflect on how God is building you up and providing you with a spiritual inheritance.

Closing Prayer

Let us pray: O God, grant that from out of the scattered nations, the confusion of many tongues may be gathered by heavenly grace into one great confession of your name. Through Jesus Christ, Our Lord. **Amen.**

Seventh Thursday of Easter

Morning Prayer

Psalm Verse

> Extol the LORD our God, **and worship at his holy mountain;**
> **for the Lord our God is holy!**
>
> —Psalm 99:9

Contemplate

God is holy, like no other, worthy of my worship due to the sheer majesty and miracle of creation alone.

Holy God, I praise you; I offer my heart to you on the heights of your eternal mountain, your heavenly places that are greater than any temple that has ever existed.

Enter the Word of God

Introduction

En route to Jerusalem, Paul is repeatedly told of negative things that will happen in Jerusalem, and people try to persuade him not to go celebrate Pentecost there. Paul eventually reaches Jerusalem and finds that there are rumors that he has been teaching people to ignore Jewish law and violating Temple rules. Some religious vigilantes even try to kill Paul (like Stephen), but the secular Roman government intervenes to maintain law and order.

✴ Scripture Reading: Acts 21:1–40 ✴

Evening Prayer

Verse to Remember

> Go, [Ananias,] for this man [Paul] is a chosen instrument of mine **to carry my name before Gentiles, kings, and Israelites.**
>
> —Acts 9:15, NABRE

Respond to God's Word

Find the important message from Agabus.

✝ Being part of God's people does not automatically erase human divisions. James and the elders of the Church in Jerusalem explain what some of the Jewish believers in Jerusalem think about Paul's missionary ministry and about gentile believers. Why do you think it is difficult for some Jews to accept gentile believers?

Meditate: Have you experienced a situation like Paul's, where your actions and words are misinterpreted, even though you go above and beyond to make yourself acceptable to your critics? Ask the Holy Spirit to give you consolation and wisdom to persevere as Paul did.

Closing Prayer

Let us pray: O God, grant that from out of the scattered nations, the confusion of many tongues may be gathered by heavenly grace into one great confession of your name. Through Jesus Christ, Our Lord. **Amen.**

Seventh Friday of Easter

Morning Prayer

Psalm Verse

> Hide your face from my sins, **and blot out all my iniquities.**
>
> —Psalm 51:9

Contemplate

Feel how effective, how wonderful, how healing, it is as God erases your sins from your heart and soul.

Jesus, merciful savior, forgive the sins I call to mind now, and blot them out so that I can cooperate more and more with your grace.

Enter the Word of God

Introduction

Paul requests to speak to the Jews in Hebrew and shares his personal testimony (with some details that we hear here for the first time). These Jews listen to Paul's speech until the moment he mentions God sending him to bring Gentiles into God's covenant.

 Scripture Reading: Acts 22:1–30 ✴

Evening Prayer

Verse to Remember

> Go, [Ananias,] for this man [Paul] is a chosen instrument of mine **to carry my name before Gentiles, kings, and Israelites.**
>
> —Acts 9:15, NABRE

Respond to God's Word

What stands out most to you from Paul's life story? See verses 1–21.

✝ Paul describes again his vivid experience of going from darkness to sight. How is any person's decision to call upon Jesus as Lord and Savior a moment that brings them new light?

 Meditate: Reflect on the role Ananias plays in Paul's life. Where in your life have you experienced or might you be called to be an "Ananias," or where might you be called to accept the care and guidance of someone like Ananias?

Closing Prayer

Let us pray: O God, grant that from out of the scattered nations, the confusion of many tongues may be gathered by heavenly grace into one great confession of your name. Through Jesus Christ, Our Lord. **Amen.**

Seventh Saturday of Easter

Morning Prayer

Psalm Verse

> They draw near who persecute me with evil purpose; they are far from your law. **But you are near, O LORD.**
>
> —Psalm 119:150–151a

Contemplate

Envision the Lord drawing near to you, especially when you experience stress, pressure, or tension with others.

God, reunite our broken human family; give me your strength and love to counter evil with your light and hope.

Enter the Word of God

Introduction

After learning that Paul is a Roman citizen with the right to a hearing, the secular government leaders want to know why Paul is under attack, and so they order the Sanhedrin to convene. As always, Paul chooses his words to connect with the council's background and viewpoints. Some have a positive response, but others plot to kill him, which causes the government to move Paul to a safer location in Caesarea.

✳ Scripture Reading: Acts 23:1–35 ✳

Evening Prayer

Verse to Remember

> Go, [Ananias,] for this man [Paul] is a chosen instrument of mine **to carry my name before Gentiles, kings, and Israelites.**
>
> —Acts 9:15, NABRE

Respond to God's Word

 What stands out to you in this passage?

✝ When speaking to the Sanhedrin, Paul tries to divide his fellow Jews based on some of their different religious beliefs. Which group of Jews do you think would be more likely to believe Jesus is the Messiah? Why?

🕯 *Meditate:* How do you think Paul felt in this situation? Maybe betrayed? Maybe as if nobody, not the Romans and not his fellow Jews, were on his side? Pray to God about a situation in your life that seems hopelessly complicated. Where can you, like Paul, still find and keep hope?

Closing Prayer

Let us pray: O God, grant that from out of the scattered nations, the confusion of many tongues may be gathered by heavenly grace into one great confession of your name. Through Jesus Christ, Our Lord. **Amen.**

Pentecost Sunday

Morning Prayer

Psalm Verse

> The LORD builds up Jerusalem; **he gathers the outcasts of Israel.**
>
> —Psalm 147:2

Contemplate

Dwell upon God's special love and his search for outcasts whom he desires to build up. In what ways or where did God once find you as an outcast?

God, you sought me and continue to seek me each and every day, to bring me back to your fold. Thank you for your everlasting love.

Enter the Word of God

Introduction

In Caesarea, the Jews accusing Paul hire a lawyer, Tertullus, to present the case against him to the governor, Felix. Paul seizes the opportunity to show the continuity between God's plan of salvation for Israel, God's Chosen People, and "the Way" now followed by the broader "Chosen People" of all believers. Felix and his wife have some interest and curiosity about Jesus the Messiah, but Felix, known as a weak administrator, avoids making a quick or definitive decision.

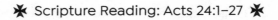 Scripture Reading: Acts 24:1–27 ✷

Evening Prayer

Verse to Remember

> You shall be my witnesses in Jerusalem **and in all Judea and Samaria and to the end[s] of the earth.**
>
> —Acts 1:8

Respond to God's Word

 Why does the Roman governor Felix keep Paul in custody for two years? See verses 26–27.

✝ In verses 14–16, Paul gives a statement of his personal beliefs and way of living them. Which phrase speaks especially to your own beliefs and living out of the Way?

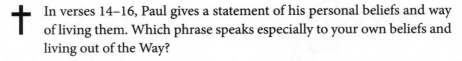 *Meditate:* Share with the Lord a situation that seems so stuck that you may have even stopped praying about it a long time ago. Ask for wisdom and patience to allow circumstances that are out of your control to slowly evolve.

Closing Prayer

Let us pray: O God, grant that from out of the scattered nations, the confusion of many tongues may be gathered by heavenly grace into one great confession of your name. Through Jesus Christ, Our Lord. **Amen.**

Monday after Pentecost

Morning Prayer

Psalm Verse

> Great is our LORD, and abundant in power; **his understanding is beyond measure.**
>
> —Psalm 147:5

Contemplate

Try to imagine the understanding of God, who is outside of time and knows the hearts of all humans. This God knows you and wills good for you.

Almighty God, I will never anticipate all of the situations you place me in, but give me comfort in knowing that you will provide the words, choices, and support I need no matter what I might face.

Enter the Word of God

Introduction

Two years later, Paul is still confined, and Festus has replaced Felix as governor (an event that happened in AD 59). The regional king, Agrippa, visits his subordinate governor, Festus, which gives Paul a chance to share God's plan and his personal story with the curious king and his wife, Bernice.

✸ Scripture Reading: Acts 25:1–26:23 ✸

Evening Prayer

Verse to Remember

> You shall be my witnesses in Jerusalem **and in all Judea and Samaria and to the end[s] of the earth.**
>
> —Acts 1:8

Respond to God's Word

 If you were Festus, what might you find challenging about this situation?

✝ How are the promises the Risen Lord made to Paul true for all of us in the Body of Christ? See Mark 26:16–18.

Meditate: How does Paul seem to deal with possible regret or remorse over his past actions, summarized in Mark 26:9–11? What does this reveal to us about God's forgiveness of sin?

Closing Prayer

Let us pray: O God, who by the mystery of the great feast of Pentecost sanctifies your whole Church in every people and nation, pour out, we pray, the gifts of the Holy Spirit across the face of the earth and, with the divine grace that was at work when the Gospel was first proclaimed, fill now once more the hearts of believers. Through Jesus Christ, Our Lord. **Amen.**

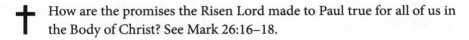

Tuesday after Pentecost

Morning Prayer

Psalm Verse

> [He] lifts the needy from the ash heap, **to make them sit with princes.**
>
> Psalm 113:7b–8a

Contemplate

Imagine how God views you, his beloved.

Lord God, to rescue me you sacrificed your only Son, and your love for me did not end in that moment. Fill me with the grace to seek your will in my life.

Enter the Word of God

Introduction

The governor and king both agree that Paul has not violated religious or secular laws. However, because Paul has used his right as a Roman citizen to make an appeal to Caesar's court, he must follow through, and so he prepares for a sea journey to Rome.

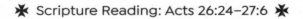 Scripture Reading: Acts 26:24–27:6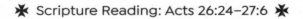

Evening Prayer

Verse to Remember

> You shall be my witnesses in Jerusalem **and in all Judea and Samaria and to the end[s] of the earth.**
>
> —Acts 1:8

Respond to God's Word

 What does Paul express disbelief at in Acts 26:26?

✝ In the Creed we proclaim that God has spoken through the prophets. What words of the prophets about Jesus stand out to you?

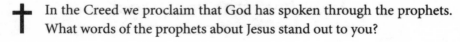 *Meditate:* In everything he does, Paul opens himself to the possibility that the Holy Spirit might use him in the conversion of someone else, even in a small way. Paul speaks with humor, personal appeal, intellect, and passion to the government officials. And he is content with the reality that conversion might be slow (see verse 29). Reflect on the role you might be playing in someone else's conversion. Ask the Holy Spirit to lead the heart of someone you know to conversion.

Closing Prayer

Let us pray: O God, who by the mystery of the great feast of Pentecost sanctifies your whole Church in every people and nation, pour out, we pray, the gifts of the Holy Spirit across the face of the earth and, with the divine grace that was at work when the Gospel was first proclaimed, fill now once more the hearts of believers. Through Jesus Christ, Our Lord. **Amen.**

Wednesday after Pentecost

Morning Prayer

Psalm Verse

> From the rising of the sun to its setting, **may the name of the Lord be praised!**
>
> —Psalm 113:3, Liturgy of the Hours translation

Contemplate

All seasons, all times of day are the Lord's. The earth is his, and our praise can rise at any moment.

Lord, give me the endurance to praise you in all situations.

Enter the Word of God

Introduction

Paul has a prophetic sense of hardship and struggle ahead on the sea journey, but Julius, the centurion in charge of him and other prisoners, ignores his warning. When circumstances become desperate, Paul encourages all by sharing a message he has received through an angel in prayer.

✠ Scripture Reading: Acts 27:7–26 ✠

Evening Prayer

Verse to Remember

> You shall be my witnesses in Jerusalem **and in all Judea and Samaria and to the end[s] of the earth.**
>
> —Acts 1:8

Respond to God's Word

 What types of planning, considerations, and concerns do you think might have gone into using sailing as an ordinary form of transportation in the first century?

 In verses 23–26, Paul shares how God spoke to him at just the right time about both trial and protection. How do trial, challenge, and even suffering fit into knowing God?

 Meditate: Have you ever experienced the long, slow, drawn-out type of waiting that Paul is experiencing over these years we are reading about? God allows such periods—think of the eons of creation prior to the moment of Jesus's Incarnation. Ask God to enter into your times of waiting.

Closing Prayer

Let us pray: O God, who by the mystery of the great feast of Pentecost sanctifies your whole Church in every people and nation, pour out, we pray, the gifts of the Holy Spirit across the face of the earth and, with the divine grace that was at work when the Gospel was first proclaimed, fill now once more the hearts of believers. Through Jesus Christ, Our Lord. **Amen.**

Thursday after Pentecost

Morning Prayer

Psalm Verse

> His delight is not in horses nor his pleasure in warriors' strength. **The Lord delights in those who revere him, in those who wait for his love.**
>
> —Psalm 147:11, Liturgy of the Hours translation

Contemplate

God delights in you, rejoices in you, not because of your achievements or good moral behavior, but because you unite your heart to him in prayer.

God, you delight in every person who turns to you, no matter their background. Thank you for this incredible love that knows no human boundaries.

Enter the Word of God

Introduction

After two weeks, the sailors and others on the ship find relief and hope as they near land. Paul urges his gentile fellow travelers to share a meal, with an allusion to the words of the Eucharist (see verse 35). Finally, the travelers make a dramatic but safe landfall on the island of Malta.

✠ Scripture Reading: Acts 27:27–44 ✠

Evening Prayer

Verse to Remember

> You shall be my witnesses in Jerusalem **and in all Judea and Samaria and to the end[s] of the earth.**
>
> —Acts 1:8

Respond to God's Word

How do both the sailors and soldiers contribute to the plan that gets everyone safely to shore?

✝ While verses 35–36 are not exactly a liturgical celebration of the Eucharist, the scene shows the power of shared meals of fellowship and giving thanks to God (even among those who are not, or not yet, believers). What does this show us about God's kingdom?

Meditate: The ship's captain and the centurion have different reactions to Paul at different points during this trip. Eventually, the centurion comes to trust Paul enough to listen to his advice. Ask the Lord to show you a situation where, although things may seem stuck, slow transformation is happening.

Closing Prayer

Let us pray: O God, who by the mystery of the great feast of Pentecost sanctifies your whole Church in every people and nation, pour out, we pray, the gifts of the Holy Spirit across the face of the earth and, with the divine grace that was at work when the Gospel was first proclaimed, fill now once more the hearts of believers. Through Jesus Christ, Our Lord. **Amen.**

Friday after Pentecost

Morning Prayer

Psalm Verse

> The LORD is high above all nations, **and his glory above the heavens!**
>
> —Psalm 113:4

Contemplate

The eternal, perfect love of Father, Son, and Spirit is beyond anything on earth. Allow this radiance, this glory, to reflect onto you.

Holy Trinity, allow me to experience your glory here on earth, and to give you glory in everything I do.

Enter the Word of God

Introduction

On Malta, gentile strangers offer Paul hospitality that vastly differs from the reception he got from his fellow Jews in Jerusalem! Three months after arriving in Malta, approximately thirty years after Jesus's Ascension, Paul arrives in the capital city of the known world, Rome, for the first time.

✳ Scripture Reading: Acts 28:1–15 ✳

Evening Prayer

Verse to Remember

> You shall be my witnesses in Jerusalem **and in all Judea and Samaria and to the end[s] of the earth.**
>
> —Acts 1:8

Respond to God's Word

What conclusions do the people on the island of Malta draw from seeing Paul getting bitten by a snake?

On Paul's journey we see all four forms of Christian prayer: blessing, petition, intercession, and thanksgiving (see *CCC*, 2623–2643). How can you apply some of these examples in your own life?

Meditate: Acts of the Apostles includes lots of movement from place to place, but behind it all is the Holy Spirit, opening and closing doors and pushing like a blowing wind to move Paul and others in the right direction. Ask God for the trust and peace you need to allow the Holy Spirit to guide your moves, even when life feels out of your control.

Closing Prayer

Let us pray: O God, who by the mystery of the great feast of Pentecost sanctifies your whole Church in every people and nation, pour out, we pray, the gifts of the Holy Spirit across the face of the earth and, with the divine grace that was at work when the Gospel was first proclaimed, fill now once more the hearts of believers. Through Jesus Christ, Our Lord. **Amen.**

Saturday after Pentecost

Morning Prayer

Psalm Verse

> Blessed be the name of the LORD **from this time forth and for evermore!**
>
> —Psalm 113:2

Contemplate

Consider God's divine providence: how you have seen it in your past and how God is already acting in your future.

Lord, you led some of your first disciples across decades in Acts of the Apostles. Stay with me, and write upon my heart the words you want me to carry as I continue the story of Acts in my own life.

Enter the Word of God

Introduction

Luke ends Acts of the Apostles in an open-ended way, not revealing whether Paul is set free and travels further west (possibly to Spain) or is martyred while in confinement in Rome under Nero's reign and persecutions. Luke highlights a scripture passage from the beginning of the prophet Isaiah's ministry, an assurance that God's plan is bigger than any human rejection and that God will continue to invite and offer salvation to all.

✖ Scripture Reading: Acts 28:16–31 ✖

Evening Prayer

Verse to Remember

> You shall be my witnesses in Jerusalem **and in all Judea and Samaria and to the end[s] of the earth.**
>
> —Acts 1:8

Respond to God's Word

 In this final location of Rome, what habits or methods of Paul's ministry do you see continuing?

 Because the New Testament has not yet been fully written and collected, Paul references the books of the Old Testament when he teaches. See verses 23–27. What are some of the most important themes of hope or promise from these books for you?

 Meditate: Reflect back on the many spiritual gifts and blessings God poured out on Paul in the Holy Spirit. Ask the Holy Spirit to come into your heart with renewed fire and to give you a spiritual gift you desire in order to live out your personal mission in life.

Closing Prayer

Let us pray: O God, who by the mystery of the great feast of Pentecost sanctifies your whole Church in every people and nation, pour out, we pray, the gifts of the Holy Spirit across the face of the earth and, with the divine grace that was at work when the Gospel was first proclaimed, fill now once more the hearts of believers. Through Jesus Christ, Our Lord. **Amen.**

THE DISCIPLES, APOSTLES, AND THE TWELVE DIAGRAM

DISCIPLE

someone who
follows a particular teacher

→ Jesus, John the Baptist, and the Pharisees all have disciples
→ Jesus has *many* more than just twelve disciples
→ even today, people who follow Jesus are called his disciples

APOSTLE

a person who is
sent out on a mission

→ Jesus sends more than twelve apostles in the New Testament
→ in a special way, bishops are successors to the apostles Jesus sent to continue his mission
→ today, all members of Christ's Body, the Church, share in the mission of being sent to spread the Kingdom of God (*CCC*, 863)

THE TWELVE

a specific, ***core group of***
Jesus's disciples/apostles
named in the New Testament

→ Mark 3:16-19; Matthew 10:2-4; Luke 6:14-16; and Acts 1:1
→ their names vary depending on the list

Next Steps

Child-Focused Ideas

This book is unique in that while it's written for adults, it can also be used by adults who desire to pray with children in the setting of a family or faith formation. As anyone who has tried to share prayer time with kids knows, it takes adaptation! Many of our assumptions and expectations of adults must shift to a place of meeting, where the child's way of relating to God is given as much importance as our own. Practical techniques for quieting oneself to prepare, incorporating movement (because sitting still is hard!), dealing with your own worry about not being able to answer questions, and more are available at colleenvermeulen.com.

Mark, Acts, What's Next?

This book is like a scaffold. You engage in the actual effort of building a habit of prayerfully reading the Bible and I share a framework to support your work. The Catholic Biblical School Ministry (catholicbiblicalschool.org), where I am Director of Mission, is an adult faith formation lay apostolate that provides similar support: expert teachers, guided plans, and questions to help Catholics like you understand the Bible and apply it to your life. We offer engaging guided tours through every book of the Bible and you can participate as an individual or by forming a group with people in your parish or community. If you grew in faith by reading the Bible along with my book, then the Catholic Biblical School Ministry approach is right for you! Prayerfully consider continuing to read additional books of the Bible, forming a group to use the Catholic Biblical School's lessons, or maybe even stepping forward to teach the Bible to others through this adult faith formation ministry.

Personal Study

Because the sacred scriptures are God's revelation of who he is and how he desires to relate to us, we are never "done" with the Bible. God always wants to meet and speak to us, his children, in his Word. To dig deeper, we need tools! Visit colleenvermeulen.com to explore some of the tools and resources that have helped me over the years. You'll find podcasts from Ave Maria Press's *Living the Word Catholic Women's Bible* series, free downloads, video presentations, frequently asked questions on tough topics, and more.

Notes

Introduction

1. Peter S. Williamson, *Ephesians* (Grand Rapids, MI: Baker Academic, 2009), 50.
2. Lavinia Spirito, "Acts: Take It to Heart," in *Living the Word Catholic Women's Bible*, ed. Sarah Christmyer (Notre Dame, IN: Ave Maria Press, 2022), 1705.

How to Use This Book

1. Maxwell Johnson, *Introduction to Benedictine Daily Prayer: A Short Breviary* (Collegeville, MN: Liturgical Press, 2015), xiii.
2. St. Gregory the Great, "Moralia (Commentary on the Book of Job)," Epistle 4, accessed October 23, 2023, https://faculty.georgetown.edu/jod/texts/moralia1.html.

Easter: Acts of the Apostles

1. Lavinia Spirito, "The Story of the Early Church," in *Living the Word Catholic Women's Bible*, ed. Sarah Christmyer (Notre Dame, IN: Ave Maria Press, 2022), 1559; cf. Acts 17:6.

Colleen Reiss Vermeulen is cofounder of catholicbiblicalschool.org and a teacher and director with the Catholic Biblical School of Michigan, an adult faith formation ministry.

After receiving her undergraduate degree from Cornell University, Vermeulen served on active duty in the US Army. She earned master of divinity and master of nonprofit administration degrees from the University of Notre Dame.

A contributing writer to the *Living the Word Catholic Women's Bible*, Colleen Vermeulen has taught children and adults the Bible for many years and served in parish catechetical, young adult, music, and evangelization ministries.

An officer in the US Army Reserve, she lives with her family in southeastern Michigan.

colleenvermeulen.com
catholicbiblicalschool.org

Sarah Christmyer is a Catholic writer, speaker, and adjunct faculty member at St. Charles Borromeo Seminary in Philadelphia, Pennsylvania. She is the codeveloper and founding editor of *The Great Adventure* Catholic Bible study program, where she served as director from 2010 to 2013. Christmyer is the general editor of the *Living the Word Catholic Women's Bible* from Ave Maria Press.

www.comeintotheword.com
Facebook: SarahChristmyer, Author
X: @SChristmyer
Instagram: @comeintotheword
Pinterest: Come Into the Word—Sarah Christmyer